Series

THE AMERICAN ANGLER GUIDE TO
WARMWATER FLY FISHING

PROVEN SKILLS, TECHNIQUES,
AND TACTICS FROM THE PROS

NATHAN PERKINSON

LYONS PRESS
GUILFORD, CONNECTICUT
An Imprint Of Globe Pequot Press

This book is dedicated to my family: Kyra, Caleb, and Samuel Perkinson;
my parents, Mike and Linda Perkinson; and Craig Perkinson,
my brother and fishing partner for the last thirty-plus years.
Thank you for all of your support!

Lyons Press is an imprint of Globe Pequot Press.

All illustrations by Robert Prince
All interior photos by Nathan Perkinson unless otherwise noted
All fly photography by Kyra Perkinson
Project editor: Staci Zacharski
Text design: Sheryl P. Kober
Layout artist: Sue Murray

Library of Congress Cataloging-in-Publication data is available on file.

ISBN 978-0-7627-9147-7

Printed in the United States of America

10 9 8 7 6 5 4 3 2 1

CONTENTS

INTRODUCTION

I distinctly remember thinking as a kid that if I had a fly rod to fish our local warmwater streams, I would only catch trout. Of course, there were no trout in the warm, rich farmland streams of southeastern Indiana, but fly rods were only for trout in my young mind. Fly fishing was high sport for adventurous mountain climbers and stuffy rich folks being paddled around by well-paid guides. To a kid who spent his summers catching redears, smallmouth, and catfish with a Zebco 33 and a 5½-foot glass rod, fly fishing was simply a foreign concept. I spent a great deal of my youth on the water, but it did not occur to me until I was grown up and married off that the same fish I caught on Hula Poppers and Rebel Crawfish would take flies.

One day I expressed a little interest in trying out fly fishing, so my wife bought me a fly-tying kit. I procured a circa-1982 ultraslow fiberglass fly rod, complete with a plastic reel and a floating line that really didn't float anymore. Game on.

Armed with crude, outdated tackle and admittedly ridiculous homemade flies, I learned to cast and to catch fish. I caught bluegills, redears, and crappies as well as largemouth and smallmouth bass. And I had a blast. Like many fly anglers, my condition worsened to the point that I moved to trout country to take on rainbows, browns, and brookies. I enjoy trout fishing, but the coldwater bug never completely took over. Even with excellent trout streams within a few miles of my house, I still get fired up when there are crappies in the shallows or I hit an especially good evening of top-water bass bugging.

As you read through this book, I hope that you will get excited at the prospect of catching warmwater fish on fly tackle. A lot of Americans live far enough from a quality coldwater fishery that a day trip for trout is out of the question, but everybody lives close enough to some river, creek, pond, or lake that is full of bluegills, bass, pike, or carp. These species and many more are ready to take your fly and give you a thrill.

If you are already an accomplished warmwater angler, I hope that I can share something new with you. If you are a coldwater angler, I would love to show you how bass and pike can be just as sporting as trout and salmon. And if you are completely new to the sport, I invite you to explore the amazing world of warmwater fly fishing with me. We'll have a look at the most popular warmwater gamefish as well as the equipment and techniques that you can use to catch them.

I'm always adding to my library of books about fly fishing, gear fishing, and tackle as well as books about fish biology and ecology. The fishing books that you accumulate will become a powerful resource and open doors to fishing adventures that you haven't even dreamed of yet. If you are only interested in freshwater fly fishing, you can still learn a lot from books about spinning or saltwater fly-fishing. Take what you learn and try it out on the water.

Don't just buy this book, thumb through it, and toss it aside. Scribble notes in the margins and dog-ear the pages that you want to come back to. Circle a few hot spots in the last chapter that you want to go fish. Toss this book in your backpack so you have something to read during sixth-period chemistry. Put it in your briefcase and look at the pictures while you're in a meeting. It doesn't matter if you live in Saint Paul or Saint Petersburg—there is great warmwater fly fishing right around the corner. Buy an expensive fly-fishing outfit if you can afford it or a cheap one if you can't. Get out there, catch some fish, and have fun!

CHAPTER 1

Know Your Warmwater Fish

It is important that you understand the habits and habitats of the warmwater gamefish that you will pursue. This knowledge will help you identify waters that hold your target species, as well as the areas in each body of water that are most likely to hold fish. As a fly angler you should also have a working knowledge of the type of prey that your quarry prefers. Fly fishing requires a great degree of deception. We voluntarily forgo the use of baits and scented lures, making it all the more important that you understand where the fish live and what they eat. The more that you know about the fish you are trying to catch, the easier it will be for you to catch them.

KEY SPECIES

The key species are the major warmwater gamefish that will likely be your main angling focus. We'll define key species as the fish that are intentionally sought for their value as sport fish or for food, while keeping the limitations of fly fishing in mind. Bass are a key species because most anglers seek them for sport, while crappies are sought for their excellent taste. I don't consider catfish a key species for fly rodders because, while they are great fighters and excellent table fare, they usually end up on the business end on a fly rod while you are out for other species.

An average largemouth bass. Notice the dark horizontal band along the fish's flank. Above this band you can clearly see the bass's lateral line, which helps the fish sense movement in the water.

Largemouth Bass

Micropterus salmoides

Range: The native range of largemouth bass is the eastern United States. However, through extensive and successful stocking programs, largemouth can now be found in every state except Alaska. You can even catch largemouth bass in southern Canada, Australia, Japan, and many European countries.

Preferred Water Temperature: Largemouth bass prefer water temperatures between 50°F and 80°F. They spawn in the spring when water temperatures are around 65°F and feed most actively when the water temperature is above 68°F.

Preferred Habitats: Largemouth bass inhabit warmwater lakes, reservoirs, ponds, and strip-mine pits as well as warmwater rivers and creeks with slow to moderate flows. Largemouth are frequently found in relation to some sort of cover or structure. They are especially fond of flooded timber, weed beds, and steep drop-offs into deep water.

Largemouth bass may be found in water with a mucky bottom, but move into rocky shallows to spawn in the spring. They are usually found in water between 1 and 20 feet deep, though extreme temperatures may drive largemouth into deeper water.

Physical Description: Largemouth bass are light green to greenish brown with a light tan or white belly and a dark unbroken horizontal band on either side. The dark band may be more evident in some populations and nearly absent in others, making positive identification of the species difficult by presence of the band alone. The jaw of a largemouth bass always extends beyond the fish's eye, so check the length of the jaw if you are unsure of the type of bass you have caught.

Average Size: Largemouth bass occupy an enormous geographical area and the size of fish can vary greatly depending on environmental conditions such as water quality, availability of food, and average annual temperature. Largemouth in the neighborhood of 2 pounds could be considered average, although fish in the 8- to 10-pound range are not uncommon. Largemouth bass can tip the scales at nearly 20 pounds in exceptional environments such as Florida, California, and Texas.

Common Food Sources: Largemouth bass will try to eat about anything that will fit into their mouths, and they have big mouths! Largemouth commonly take smaller fish, crayfish, leeches, frogs, and mice. They may eat nymphs and surface insects on occasion, but you can put away your tiny trout flies because it usually takes a mouthful to tempt old bucketmouth. Largemouth bass are opportunistic feeders and are often most active in the early morning and late evening. As water temperatures drop below 60°F, largemouth continue to feed, although they become sluggish and are less likely to move very far for a meal.

Note: Largemouth bass are often the first large gamefish that we encounter, regardless of the type of tackle we use. The range of largemouth is vast, and the species can literally be found from coast to coast.

Largemouth bass are tolerant of water ranging from cool and clear to warm and murky. They are not selective feeders and will readily take both top-water and subsurface flies. Largemouth bass do not make long runs like trout or salmon, but do not discount their fighting ability. Even a modest-size largemouth will put a serious bend in your fly rod and fight with stubborn tenacity. Sharpen your hooks, check your leader, and get ready for a vicious, head-shaking battle when you go after these greenback monsters.

Smallmouth Bass
Micropterus dolomieui

Smallmouth bass have dark vertical bars rather than horizontal lines like largemouth bass.

Range: Smallmouth bass may be found from southern Canada well into the southern United States, including parts of northern Georgia, Alabama, and Arkansas. Smallmouth range as far west as Texas and Oklahoma and have been stocked in other western waters, though not with the same success as largemouth bass.

Preferred Water Temperature: Smallmouth bass prefer slightly cooler water than largemouth bass, though not nearly as cool as you may have been led to believe. Unlike trout, which slow down or stop feeding as water temperatures climb out of their comfort range, smallmouth actively feed when water temperatures are above 67°F and they continue to feed (and take flies) as water temperatures rise into the 80°F range. Smallies can be coaxed into taking a fly when water temperatures are in the low 50s, and we will cover some special techniques for cool-water smallmouth in the bass chapter. They spawn in the spring when water temperatures are around 64°F.

Preferred Habitats: Smallmouth bass live in creeks and rivers with moderate currents as well as some deep lakes. Smallmouth are most often found over rocky bottoms or near rocky structure or cover, but they will take advantage of woody cover like fallen timber and submerged logs if it is available. Rocky riffles, stone outcroppings, and gravel bottoms are prime smallmouth lies. Smallmouth bass are not as likely to be found hiding in aquatic vegetation as largemouth bass, though they will take cover in weeds if nearby water conditions are favorable.

Physical Description: Smallmouth bass are olive green to brown with silvery yellow or white bellies. Smallmouth bass may be distinguished from largemouth bass by several dark vertical bands on the back and sides, rather than the dark horizontal bands worn by largemouth bass. Smallmouth also have three distinct dark bands that radiate from the nose, through the eyes, and across the gill plates. These bands are sometimes visible on largemouth bass, but are nearly always evident on smallmouth bass. As you might guess, smallmouth bass have smaller mouths than largemouth bass. You can easily discern a smallmouth by the length of the jaw, which extends to, but not beyond, the fish's eye.

Average Size: Smallmouth bass do not grow as big as their largemouth cousins, averaging about 1½ pounds. Larger fish up to 3 or 4 pounds are common in quality fisheries, and smallmouth over 5 pounds are considered trophies. Smallmouth bass grow quickly in the southern reaches of their range, but are short-lived. In northern climates a trophy-size smallmouth may be fifteen years old, so bear in mind the probable age of a nice northern bronzeback before you commit it to the frying pan. These prized fish are a real treasure that should be released whenever possible.

Common Food Sources: Smallmouth bass seem to prefer crayfish over any other food source, but they are far from selective. Baitfish, leeches, and insect larvae are also on the menu, as well as top-water morsels like frogs and crippled baitfish. Like the largemouth, smallmouth bass will strike any fly that somewhat resembles a food source.

Note: Smallmouth bass are real aquatic acrobats that will delight you with their splashy aerial displays and powerful fighting style. They inhabit many of the same types of water as do trout, and may be found in the lower stretches of trout streams. It is not uncommon to catch smallmouth bass and brown trout from the same water, which has given rise to the popular misconception that smallmouth, like trout, stop feeding as water temperatures near the 80°F mark. In fact, late-summer smallmouth bass fishing can be incredible when water temperatures are above the ideal trout range. Rather than give up on late-summer smallmouth, look for streams with rocky bottoms and lots of cover to catch the best bronzebacks of the season. Big smallmouth bass will aggressively take top-water and subsurface offerings, and landing these bronze battlers on fly gear will definitely test your angling skills.

Crappie

Pomoxis nigromaculatus, black crappie
Pomoxis annularis, white crappie

Crappies are typically larger and more elongated than bluegills. KYRA PERKINSON

Range: The native range of crappies included most of the Ohio River and Mississippi River drainages. However, these prolific gamefish have been successfully introduced across North America.

Preferred Water Temperature: Both black and white crappies seek water temperatures in the 70°F to 75°F range. However, your best shot at crappies with a fly rod will probably occur in the spring when water temperatures are between 48°F and 60°F. Crappies move into shallow water to spawn when the water hits 48°F and actually begin spawning at 60°F. This period of pre-spawn staging and spawning will provide the best opportunity of the year to put a fly in front of these aggressive fish.

Preferred Habitats: Both types of crappies may be found in lakes, reservoirs, creeks, and rivers. White crappies are more tolerant of murky water than black crappies. Both species seem to prefer clear water where there is ample aquatic vegetation for cover. Post-spawn crappies

7

congregate around subsurface cover like fallen timber and man-made structure such as "fish cribs."

Physical Description: Aside from the black bass, which are technically part of the sunfish family, crappies are the largest sunfish. Crappies have thin, delicate mouth membranes, earning them the common nickname "papermouth." White crappies have silvery sides with dark vertical bars and elongated heads. Black crappies have dark spots rather than distinct vertical bars and have shorter heads than white crappies.

Average Size: Across their range, crappies average about 8 inches in length, or about ¾ pound. Larger "slabs" up to 3 pounds may be caught, especially around spawning time.

Common Food Sources: Crappies are primarily fish-eaters, though they sometimes take crayfish, insects, and larvae.

Note: Crappies are highly sought for their sweet white meat. They will aggressively take flies, but are not strong fighters. Set the hook on a crappie with a solid strip-strike and land the fish by hand or in a net. If you try to lift a crappie from the water by the hook or leader, you run the risk of tearing its mouth and losing the fish. Crappies are easy to locate in the spring when the spawning run is under way, but they quickly retreat to open water where they school and suspend at middle depths. This can make crappies frustratingly difficult to locate during the summer. Identifying structure and cover is the key to summer crappie success.

Bluegill
Lepomis macrochirus

Range: The native range of bluegills included most waters between the Rocky Mountains and the Atlantic Ocean, with the exception of the Northeast. The bluegill is now common in nearly every body of water across the continent.

Bluegills are small, saucer-shaped fish that readily take flies.

Preferred Water Temperature: Bluegills will actively seek water temperatures between 75°F and 80°F. They spawn in the spring when water temperatures are around 69°F.

Preferred Habitats: Bluegills can be found in nearly any pond, lake, river, or creek. There are certain environmental factors that produce the largest bluegills, however. Moderate weed growth in a warmwater lake favors big bluegills, as the weeds provide bluegill cover as well as a substrate that produces insect larvae, baitfish, and other foods favored by bluegills. Access to deep water is another important point to consider when you are searching for big bluegills. Shallow bays in lakes and reservoirs often hold many bluegills, but they are usually uniformly sized, stunted fish. The largest bluegills seek the shelter of deep water and only come into the shallows to spawn or feed. If you are going to concentrate on shallow areas or spawning fish, be sure that there is deep water for larger bluegills nearby.

The overall number of bluegills in a given body of water can also affect the size of the fish. Bluegills reproduce at a prolific rate and can quickly overpopulate a lake. This is a common problem in lakes and reservoirs that lack sufficient predation to keep the bluegill population in check. The end result is a lake filled with massive numbers of small bluegills that are of little interest to anglers. For this reason, look for lakes that are known to have a healthy population of predator species like pike, bass, and walleye. These lakes will have the best bluegill populations as well.

Physical Description: Bluegills are saucer-shaped panfish. They are olive green in color with dark vertical bars on the sides. The edge of the gill cover has a light bluish hue, giving the fish its common name. Bluegills have dull reddish-orange breasts that become bright and vivid on males during spawning time. Many varieties of panfish, including pumpkinseeds, redbreast sunfish, and redears, are mistakenly categorized as "bluegills." True bluegills will always have the powder-blue coloration on their gill covers and solid-black gill cover lobes.

Average Size: The average size of bluegills is about 5 to 6 inches long. Larger fish are common when conditions are favorable. Hand-size bluegills are a good catch and can weigh over 1 pound, while a 2-pound bluegill is a real prize.

Common Food Sources: Like many panfish, bluegills have tiny mouths and take smaller food than bass and crappies. Aquatic insects, larvae, and tiny baitfish are common bluegill food. Bluegills are very aggressive feeders, though, so don't be surprised when a 6-inch bluegill tries to take on your size 2 bass bug!

Note: If you have ever cast a fly, retrieved a lure, or floated worms under a bobber, you have probably caught some bluegills. Although considered child's play by some anglers, catching bluegills is just plain fun. You can always count on bluegills to take any fly and to fight like little devils when you set the hook. As an added bonus, you don't have to feel too guilty about keeping a few bluegills, and they are excellent either baked or fried.

INCIDENTAL SPECIES

By incidental species, I mean gamefish that are likely to be caught while you are targeting a key species, or fish that are not at the forefront of fly fishing because of geographic limitations. The importance of these species to their respective environments, not to mention their value as sport fish, does not make them incidental; it is just that they exist in the periphery of most fly anglers' minds. You can still have a great time walking along a wooded creek and catching green sunfish all day, even though that would not qualify as "sport" fishing in some circles.

Spotted "Kentucky" Bass
Micropterus punctulatus

Range: Spotted bass range a bit farther than their nickname implies. Kentucky is prime spotted bass country, though they may be found in pockets throughout much of the Mississippi River and Ohio River drainages. Like the smallmouth bass, spotted bass are not as tolerant of unfavorable water conditions as largemouth bass. As a result, spotted bass have not been widely stocked outside their native range.

Preferred Water Temperature: Spotted bass feed most actively when the water temperature is around 75°F. They spawn in spring as water temperatures reach 65°F.

Preferred Habitats: Spotted bass thrive in clear creeks and rivers with moderate flow. They may also be found in reservoirs where there is access to deep water. Like other black bass, spotted bass are often found in relation to underwater structure and hiding in and around submerged cover.

Physical Description: Spotted bass are usually smaller than either smallmouth or largemouth bass. They are olive green to copper brown in color with a broken horizontal line of spots along both sides and dark spots on the back. The jaw of a spotted bass extends to the rear of the eye, somewhat longer than that of a smallmouth bass. Spotted bass may easily be mistaken for largemouth bass, though the presence of a tooth patch on the tongue will correctly identify your fish as a spotted bass.

Average Size: Spotted bass average about 12 inches in length, with a typical fish weighing about 1 pound.

Common Food Sources: Crayfish, baitfish, and large insect larvae make up a significant portion of the spotted bass's diet. Like other black bass, spotted bass are nonselective feeders and will attempt to take about any food source that will fit in their mouths.

Note: Spotted bass look somewhat like a cross between largemouth and smallmouth bass, though they are actually a separate species. What the spotted bass lacks in size, it makes up for with stunning coloration and markings. These fish are feisty fighters and will readily take flies. Spotted bass inhabit some of the most scenic streams in the eastern United States. If you like catching beautiful fish in picturesque waters, you will appreciate the spotted bass.

Rock Bass
Ambloplites rupestris

Range: The rock bass is native to the eastern United States, from the Great Lakes south to northern Georgia and Alabama and west to the Mississippi River.

Preferred Water Temperature: Rock bass are most active when water temperatures are between 69°F and 74°F. They spawn in the spring when water temperatures reach 68°F.

Rock bass are among the many types of panfish that are eager to take flies.

Preferred Habitats: Rock bass live in clean lakes and streams with moderate flow. True to their name, rock bass are usually found over rocky bottoms and around rocky outcroppings or rock piles. Rock bass can frequently be caught under and around docks.

Physical Description: Rock bass vary in color from light brown to green depending on their surroundings. They have several horizontal rows of dark spots on the sides. Rock bass have large reddish-brown eyes that protrude from the sides of the head, earning them the common nickname "goggle-eyes."

Average Size: Rock bass fall between black bass and panfish in size, with an average fish about 7 inches in length. They are broad, somewhat pan-shaped fish that can easily reach 1 to 1½ pounds.

Common Food Sources: Rock bass feed on small fish, crayfish, and insect larvae. They are aggressive feeders and will strike any fly.

Note: Rock bass are of a separate genus from the other common black bass. They do not grow as big as largemouth or smallmouth bass, but are generally larger than most panfish from the same water. Rock bass are very aggressive and capable of taking large top-water and subsurface flies. They are frequently caught while fishing for largemouth or smallmouth bass in eastern waters and may be considered a nuisance. On the other hand, it is pretty easy to fill a stringer with rock bass when nothing else is biting, and they are good for fish fries.

Yellow Perch
Perca flavescens

Range: Yellow perch are native to the United States and Canada east of the Rocky Mountains, though they have been introduced to nearly every state and province.

Preferred Water Temperature: Yellow perch are active in water temperatures up to about 72°F. They spawn in spring when water temperatures reach 43°F.

Preferred Habitats: Yellow perch are found in sparsely vegetated lakes. The largest perch are usually caught in deeper water than the smaller ones.

Physical Description: Yellow perch are yellowish to olive green with several distinctive vertical bands on each side. The pelvic fins on yellow perch are reddish orange.

Average Size: Yellow perch average about 9 inches in length and may reach 1½ to 2 pounds.

Common Food Sources: Yellow perch feed on smaller fish and aquatic invertebrates such as freshwater shrimp.

Note: Yellow perch are a very popular gamefish among bait anglers. As members of the walleye family, they are second to none in terms of food quality. Yellow perch are usually caught with bait, but may be caught on fly tackle when you are targeting bluegills and other panfish.

Catfish and Bullheads

Catfish and bullheads are common in nearly all warmwater creeks, rivers, lakes, and reservoirs east of the Rocky Mountains. They are easily identified by the barbels, or "whiskers," around their mouths, as well as their smooth skin. Members of the catfish family are highly regarded among bait anglers for their size, fighting ability, and table quality. Although generally considered strict bottom-feeders, catfish will take baitfish both on the bottom and in the middle depths of the water column. They may strike at streamers, jig flies, and even egg flies. That said, specifically targeting catfish with fly tackle can be a difficult proposition because catfish rely heavily on their sense of smell when feeding. These heavyweight fighters are most likely to wind up on your line as an incidental catch.

SPECIAL TARGETS

Special targets are warmwater species that require special equipment or techniques to consistently catch due to their size, their habits, or their habitats. Special target species may be caught incidentally while fishing for other species, but the dedicated pursuit of these fish calls for an in-depth knowledge of their behaviors, habitats, and feeding preferences that goes beyond general angling competence. Catching striped bass in freshwater requires special techniques because stripers live in open water.

Likewise, the pursuit of trophy-size pike and muskellunge also requires special tackle and flies because these fish are so large and powerful.

Striped Bass
Morone saxatilis

Striped bass are saltwater fish that thrive in large freshwater reservoirs. They are torpedo-shaped with distinct dark lines along their flanks. JIM KLUG

Range: Striped bass are anadromous fish, native to the saltwater coasts of the eastern United States. In their native saltwater habitat, they enter freshwater rivers only to spawn. Although a saltwater species, striped bass are capable of living their entire lives in freshwater and have been stocked in reservoirs and large river systems throughout the United States.

Preferred Water Temperature: Striped bass prefer water temperatures between 65°F and 75°F. They feed actively when water temperatures are above 50°F. Stripers often hang around the thermocline, or the delineation between warm and cool water, in large lakes. From there, they can stalk and attack baitfish in the warmer water above. Striped bass spawn when water temperatures reach 55°F, though spawning in large reservoirs may be limited due to a lack of suitable habitat.

Preferred Habitats: Striped bass are open-water fish, unlike largemouth and smallmouth bass, which relate to some type of structure or cover. Much of their time is spent schooling or patrolling deep, open water for baitfish.

Physical Description: Striped bass are long, sleek fish with silver sides. Several horizontal stripes extend from the gill plate to the tail. The horizontal stripes may be broken, especially below the lateral line. Striped bass have two tooth patches on the tongue, which can be used to positively identify your catch.

Average Size: Striped bass average about 25 inches in length, and 10-pound fish are not uncommon.

Common Food Sources: Striped bass eat baitfish like threadfin shad and gizzard shad.

Note: The striped bass is an amazing gamefish, eager to eat flies and capable of putting up an extraordinary fight. Locating striped bass is the key to catching them, as freshwater stripers are often found cruising the vast, featureless depths of large reservoirs. Striped bass are as formidable a target as any freshwater angler could hope for and can bring the excitement of catching a genuine saltwater sport fish to the average warmwater angler. If you plan on pursuing these powerful fish, you will need to invest in some heavy fly tackle.

White Bass
Morone chrysops

Range: White bass are native to the midwestern United States, generally within the drainages of the Great Lakes and the Ohio and Mississippi

Rivers. They have been successfully stocked throughout much of the United States and Canada today.

Preferred Water Temperature: White bass prefer water temperatures between 65°F and 75°F. They spawn in the spring when water temperatures reach 58°F.

Preferred Habitats: White bass are found in large reservoirs and rivers. They are schooling, open-water fish that do not typically relate to any specific structure or cover.

Physical Description: White bass are white to silvery in color with several broken or irregular dark horizontal lines on the sides. Though they resemble striped bass, they are not as elongated as their anadromous cousins.

Average Size: White bass average about 12 inches in length and around 1½ to 2 pounds.

Common Food Sources: White bass eat smaller baitfish. They feed in mass frenzies, often causing the water's surface to boil with activity as baitfish try to escape.

Note: White bass do not grow as large as striped bass, but they are a popular sport fish in their own right. Fishing for white bass in open water requires a boat and a keen eye to pick up on signs of feeding activity. Once you are on a feeding frenzy the action can be fast, with a hookup on every cast.

Northern Pike
Esox lucius

Range: Northern pike may be found in the United States and Canada, generally north of the Ohio River and within the Missouri River

Northern pike are long, muscular fish with flat heads and large mouths. Look for light spots on a dark background to differentiate pike from muskellunge. CHAD RAICH

drainage. They have been successfully stocked in many western reservoirs, and some anglers consider the pike a threat to native species in the West. Northern pike are one of the few freshwater fish that are native to North America, Europe, and Asia.

Preferred Water Temperature: Northern pike prefer water temperatures in the range of 50°F to 70°F. With such a wide range of favorable temperatures, pike may be found in both warmwater bass streams and coldwater trout streams. Although they are tolerant of warm water, the biggest pike will seek the cooler water of springs, feeder creeks, and undercut bank as the temperature rises.

Preferred Habitats: Northern pike may be found in lakes, marshes, large rivers, and creeks. They are ambush predators and are often found hiding in heavy cover such as fallen timber and thick weed beds.

Physical Description: Northern pike are large, long fish with flat heads. They are olive green with many oval-shaped tan spots. Northern pike have light spots on a dark background, while the similar muskellunge has dark spots on a light background. Pike have enormous mouths and very sharp teeth.

Average Size: Northern pike average about 24 inches in length and around 5 pounds, though much larger pike are common.

Common Food Sources: Like bass, northern pike will eat anything that will fit in their mouths. Smaller fish, frogs, and even birds are common prey for pike.

Note: Northern pike are a common gamefish throughout much of the northern United States. They can tolerate a wide range of water temperature and quality, making them a readily accessible big-game species for many warmwater anglers. Small pike under 24 inches can be caught on fairly standard fly tackle, but going after trophy-size fish will require wire leaders, giant flies, and a heavy rod and reel.

Muskellunge
Esox masquinongy

Range: Muskellunge may be found in the eastern United States and Canada, from the Great Lakes south to Tennessee and South Carolina.

Preferred Water Temperature: Muskellunge are most active when water temperatures are around 70°F.

Preferred Habitats: Muskellunge are usually found in the weedy cover of lakes and large, slow rivers.

Physical Description: Like northern pike, muskellunge are large, long fish with flat heads and many sharp teeth. Identification of a muskellunge can be difficult, as there are several color phases in addition to muskellunge-pike hybrids. Muskellunge are typically olive to silvery green in color, with many dark spots on the back and sides. Barred muskellunge feature solid stripes on their flanks, while clear muskellunge have no spots or bars at all. Muskellunge-pike hybrids are striped as well and are called "tiger muskellunge." If you wish to positively identify your catch as a muskellunge, look at the underside of the fish's lower jaw. There are between twelve and eighteen pores on the lower jaw of a muskellunge, whereas pike have ten or fewer pores.

Average Size: Muskellunge average about 35 inches in length and may grow much larger. They average about 12 pounds, though 40-pound fish are not uncommon.

Common Food Sources: Muskellunge eat smaller fish as well as frogs, mice, and birds. Keep in mind that "smaller fish" may be quite large as far as muskies are concerned.

Note: The muskellunge may be the most challenging warmwater fish for fly anglers. Not only are muskellunge far less common than northern pike, they seem to tease anglers with their selectivity. Muskellunge are difficult to locate and like to chase flies over long distances before striking. Often a perfect presentation to a muskie will result in nothing but a follow and flat refusal at the boat side. The muskellunge has a reputation as the "fish of ten thousand casts," and there are days when it certainly lives up to that moniker.

Common Carp
Cyprinus carpio

Range: The common carp may be found in every state except Alaska.

Preferred Water Temperature: Carp are most active when water temperatures are between 69°F and 80°F. They spawn when water temperatures are around 62°F.

Carp are golden brown in color with large scales. They feed on a variety of foods including aquatic plants, fruits, insects, and baitfish. HENRY COWEN

Preferred Habitats: Carp may be found in rivers, creeks, lakes, reservoirs, and ponds. They are often found around aquatic vegetation or over soft, mucky bottoms.

Physical Description: The common carp is a big fish, easily identified by its large scales and the pair of barbels around its mouth.

Average Size: Carp average about 20 inches in length and around 5 pounds. Much larger fish are common, and 40-pound carp are considered trophies.

Common Food Sources: Carp are omnivorous, meaning that they eat both plants and animals. They often feed near the bottom, stirring up small invertebrates such as insect larvae and freshwater shrimp.

Note: The common carp has been much maligned over the years. Once considered lowly bottom-feeders and trash fish (let's not forget, trout feed on the bottom as well), carp have now attained a cultlike following among a growing circle of dedicated fly anglers. The truth is that carp are selective feeders, are exceptionally aware of their environment, and are downright difficult to catch on a fly. Add to that the fact that hooking a carp is somewhat akin to hooking the world's largest bonefish, and you have a challenging sport fish indeed.

PANFISH: REDEAR SUNFISH, GREEN SUNFISH, REDBREAST SUNFISH, LONGEAR SUNFISH, AND PUMPKINSEED

There are many species of panfish that may be found in the same water as the popular bluegill. The habits and habitats of these panfish may differ slightly, but they share enough common traits and preferences that there is no appreciable difference when you are fly fishing for them.

Some panfish are worth catching just so that you can look at them. Although they do not reach the same trophy sizes as trout, pumpkinseeds are gorgeous fish worthy of snapping a photo or two. Green sunfish are lovely, too, with long streaks of turquoise radiating from the cheeks. If you are looking for a fight, try targeting redear sunfish. These scrappy brawlers will put a bend in your rod, and you will swear that you have hooked a fish twice as big.

These panfish are often thrown into the bluegill category, but there are actually several species of common panfish. Many are small, though large specimens certainly occur. If you find yourself looking at a slow day of bass fishing, tie on a beat-up old wet fly and try catching some panfish. You will feel like a kid again, guaranteed.

CHAPTER 2

Warmwater Fly-Fishing Equipment

Warmwater fly fishing can be as simple or as complicated as you wish. Whether you are shopping for your first fly-fishing outfit or looking to add to your collection, it is helpful to know what equipment you need to pursue warmwater sport fish. Fortunately, we live in an age where anglers can expect high-quality fly rods, lines, and reels at very modest prices. Let's have a look at what you will need to get started and a few extras that are nice to have on the water.

FLY RODS

Graphite fly rods dominate the market today, and for good reason. Graphite rods are strong, durable, and easy to cast. You can expect good casting and fighting quality from many entry-level graphite fly rods.

There are several factors that determine the performance of a fly rod. The first is the rod's designated weight. The designated weight of a fly rod has little to do with how much the rod actually weighs. The weight is a number that refers to the line weight that the rod is designed to cast most efficiently. For example, a 5-weight fly rod will best cast a 5-weight fly line. In some cases you may wish to size up your line, say by casting a 6-weight line with a 5-weight rod. This overloads the rod, making it easier to cast the line. On the other hand, trying to cast a 4-weight line with a 5-weight rod will be very difficult, so be sure that your rod and line weights are at least even, if not heavier on the line side.

Popular fly-rod weights for warmwater fishing range from 4-weight for panfish to 10-weight for striped bass. If you are starting to build a warmwater fly-fishing outfit for all-around bass fishing, an 8-weight graphite rod is a good place to start.

Another factor to consider when shopping for fly rods is the length. Common fly-rod lengths are between 7½ to 9½ feet. A longer rod will allow you to cast farther and will extend your reach, making it easier to mend and pick up line. In some cases, such as fishing small streams with a canopy of foliage overhead, you may prefer a shorter rod. A shorter rod can make casting in tight quarters easier, although short rods limit your casting distance and reach. A 9-foot rod is standard fare and will serve you well in most warmwater fly-fishing situations, whether you fish on streams or open water.

"Rod action" is the term used to describe how much of the rod bends when you are casting fly line. If the fly rod only bends toward the tip, the rod has a fast action. If the rod bends deeply toward the grip when you cast, the rod has a slow action. Most graphite rods produced today have a moderate to fast actions, which makes it a lot easier to cast the large flies that are used for warmwater fly fishing. Moderate-fast graphite fly rods are more forgiving to beginners who are learning to cast. As you put together your first warmwater fly-fishing outfit, look for a moderate-fast to fast-action graphite fly rod. Fiberglass and bamboo rods usually have slower actions, making it more difficult to cast large flies, and are not as easy to cast when you are just starting out.

FLY REELS

Fly reels were once considered secondary pieces of equipment, little more than a place to store extra line. A basic, inexpensive fly reel will certainly hold your line and will work for many warmwater species.

However, there are some really fantastic fly reels on the market today which feature drag systems that will help you to control and land strong-running fish.

Ratchet-and-pawl drags slow the line as it is being pulled from the reel through the use of a clicker and a gear. This is a common, inexpensive alternative to disc-drag systems. A fly reel with a basic ratchet-and-pawl drag system will work for most warmwater fly fishing. If you plan to fish for largemouth and smallmouth bass or panfish, a ratchet-and-pawl drag system will work fine. These fish run hard but not very far, so you can usually control the fish without employing an elaborate drag system.

Disc-drag systems use the friction between internal disc surfaces to slow the line. This produces a very smooth drag that helps to control the line and place more pressure on the fish. Disc-drag systems can be expensive, but if you plan to fish for striped bass, carp, and other fish that run long and fast, you will appreciate the control that a disc-drag system offers.

The fly rod and line work together to allow you to cast lightweight flies. You can see the moderate-fast action of this rod, as only the upper third bends. KYRA PERKINSON

FLY LINES

Unlike monofilament spinning and bait-casting lines, fly lines are weighted. This is what allows you to cast an essentially weightless fly great distances. Spin-fishing lines are rated according to their breaking strength, but fly lines are rated by a weight system that is determined by the actual weight of the first 30 feet of the line. Fly line weights are designated by a number usually between 1 and 12, with heavier specialty lines available. Lighter lines are assigned lower numbers.

For warmwater fly fishing, you should at least match your fly line weight to the designated weight of your fly rod. Stringing up line that is one or two sizes heavier than your rod weight is even better for casting bulky bass bugs and heavy streamers. Take into consideration your own casting skills as well as the size and type of flies that you will be casting before you purchase a preloaded combination kit with a rod, reel, and line. You may save a few bucks by going with the kit, but an even-weight or undersized line can make it more difficult to cast large flies.

Fly lines are treated in various ways to produce different results when you cast. Floating lines float on the water's surface and are useful for fishing both top-water flies and swimming streamers within a few feet of the surface. Sinking lines contain extra weight that causes the line to sink at a specific rate, making them the best choice when fish are holding deep.

Fly lines also feature different tapers that will affect their casting performance. Level fly lines are inexpensive and basically useless if you are casting flies of any size. You should avoid them for warmwater fly fishing. Double-taper fly lines feature identically tapered sections at both ends. These lines are ideal for delicate spring-creek trout presentations, but are still a bit undersized for most warmwater fly fishing.

Weight-forward fly lines are the best choice for warmwater fly fishing. Some weight-forward lines are actually marketed as "bass bug" tapers. Weight-forward fly lines have the line weight concentrated toward the front of the line, making it much easier to accurately cast bass bugs and large streamers.

You may be surprised to learn that most fly lines are less than 100 feet long. That does not leave much room for fighting fish, so it is necessary to add backing to the line. The backing is a high-strength level line that is wound on the reel before the fly line then attached to the fly line with a knot. The size of your reel will determine how much backing you can carry. Most fly reels will accommodate about 300 feet of backing, which is plenty to keep you from losing a fish should it run out the entire length of your fly line.

LEADERS AND TIPPETS

Fly lines are much too heavy to present flies, so it is necessary to have a leader between the fly line and the fly. Monofilament nylon and fluorocarbon are the most common leader materials. Monofilament holds knots well, is inexpensive, and will not sink your fly. It should be your first choice for top-water fly fishing in warm water. Fluorocarbon is very resistant to abrasion and sinks in water, clearly making it a favorite leader material for fishing subsurface warmwater flies.

Monofilament or fluorocarbon leaders provide a connection between your heavy fly line and the fly itself. KYRA PERKINSON

While delicate presentations are necessary when you are casting size 20 dry flies to rising trout, most warmwater fly-fishing presentations are less subtle. You do not need a long, fine leader to fish for warmwater species. Manufactured "knotless" leaders are great for warmwater fly fishing because they have no knots to pick up algae and weeds. When you are fishing bass bugs or surface flies, you may clip the tippet section off of a knotless leader until it is about 6 or 7 feet long. A knotless leader trimmed this way is heavy enough to punch bulky bass bugs through the air and will still provide enough separation between your fly and the fly line to avoid spooking fish.

Weighted subsurface flies may be cast using knotless tapered leaders, though a level length of fluorocarbon is even better. Fluorocarbon will sink along with the fly and is tough enough to hold up in the rough underwater of warmwater fish. Unless you are casting light streamers to spooky warmwater fish, like carp, you do not need a tapered fluorocarbon leader. The weight of a heavy subsurface fly is enough to turn over a level leader.

Northern pike and muskellunge have a lot of sharp teeth and can bite or tear through a normal fly leader. If you are fishing for pike or

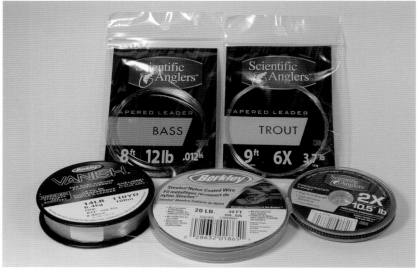

A variety of leader materials: knotless tapered bass and trout leaders, fluorocarbon, nylon-coated wire for pike and muskies, and monofilament tippet.

muskies, you should buy or make a few "bite tippets." A bite tippet is a length of heavy monofilament or supple wire that attaches the fly to the leader. You can certainly land pike and muskellunge with standard leaders, but adding a bite tippet will throw the odds in your favor.

KNOTS

There are hundreds of knots than can be used in all sorts of fly-fishing situations, but these few simple, strong knots are really all that you will need.

Clinch Knot

The clinch knot is used to attach the fly to the leader. The clinch knot is strong enough to hold fish, but may slip if your fly becomes snagged.

Palomar Knot

The Palomar knot is another fly-to-leader knot. A Palomar knot will not slip, but requires the entire fly to be passed through a loop in the knot. This can waste a lot of leader material, so avoid tying Palomar knots if you plan on changing flies often. Use the Palomar knot for large game-fish like largemouth bass, northern pike, and striped bass.

Duncan Loop or Uni-Knot

The Duncan loop is an alternative fly-to-leader knot. A Duncan loop can easily be tied through the eye of a fly. The Duncan will hold your fly securely while allowing plenty of room for the fly to move. Use the Duncan loop to attach subsurface streamers to your leader. The Uni-Knot system is a series of knots that allows you to cover all sorts of situations by modifying the standard Duncan loop.

Double Surgeon's Knot

The double surgeon's knot is the simplest way to attach two sections

of leader material. It is handy for adding tippet material if you have changed flies a few times or if you are tying your own tapered leaders.

Perfection Loop

The perfection loop cannot be tied through the eye of a hook, but it is useful for making loops in leaders. These loops may be used to quickly change out leaders by passing them through a loop on the end of your fly line. You can tie a loop on the end of your fly line with fly-tying

thread or purchase manufactured loop-ends that glue onto the line. Some trout anglers shun this practice, but loop-to-loop connections have little impact on casting and presenting bass bugs and big streamers. Quick-change loop-to-loop connections also beat the heck out of tying nail knots on the water!

Albright Knot

The Albright knot is used to securely attach two lines when there is a great difference in diameter between the lines. An Albright knot

is rather large and bulky, but it is the best way to tie a bite tippet to your leader.

FLIES

The flies that you use for warmwater fly fishing will be determined by the species you target, the conditions you are facing, and the type of water you are fishing. Let's have a look at the basic types of flies that should be in your warmwater fly-fishing box.

Bass Bugs

Bass bugs are the large top-water flies that are used to catch largemouth and smallmouth bass as well as pike and muskellunge. Bass bugs can be made from spun-and-clipped deer hair, balsa wood, or foam. A popper is a bass bug with a flat face that pushes water when retrieved. A slider is a bass bug that is smoothly tapered toward the front so that it slides along the surface, gently diving when retrieved. A diver is a tapered bass bug with a high collar that dives deep and causes a lot of disturbance when retrieved. Bass bugs will range from size 4 to size 2/0 or larger depending on the species you are pursuing. We will get into fly sizes in greater detail in the species chapters.

Panfish Poppers

"Panfish popper" is a general term that describes top-water flies used for panfish. You can tie deer-hair poppers, fashion poppers from foam or balsa, or purchase manufactured poppers. Many panfish poppers have rubber legs and feather tails to lure panfish into striking. Sizes 6 through 12 should cover all of your panfish popper needs.

Wet Flies

Traditional wet flies are very useful for catching subsurface panfish. Soft-hackle and winged wet flies in sizes 6 through 12 are effective panfish flies.

Dry Flies

Panfish will take dry flies as well. You can tie a handful of dry flies or just use some beat-up flies that have already seen service on a trout stream. Panfish will eagerly rise to standard dry flies and parachute flies. Sizes 10 through 16 are best for tiny panfish mouths.

Swimming Streamers

Swimming streamers are non-weighted or lightly weighted streamer flies that are fished in the water column rather than on the bottom. Swimming streamers can imitate baitfish, leeches, and crayfish. In many cases, the only difference between a swimming streamer and a bottom streamer is the amount of weight that has been added to the fly. Hook size is secondary to the overall size of the fly where warmwater streamers are concerned. Swimming streamers in the 3- to 6-inch range are good for most warmwater species.

Bottom Streamers

Bottom streamers are weighted to fish on or near the bottom. These streamers are used to imitate bottom-dwelling crayfish, sculpins, and madtoms. Adding off-center weight to bottom streamers produces a jigging action that is very effective for subsurface bass. As with swimming streamers, the overall size of the fly is more important than the hook size. We'll have a closer look at bottom streamers and specific techniques in the species chapters.

STRIKE INDICATORS

The use of strike indicators is taboo in many angling circles. Often dismissed as "bobbers," strike indicators are actually excellent tools that will help you pick up on the lightest strikes. Strike indicators are an important part of many proven warmwater fly-fishing techniques. We will cover some techniques that use strike indicators as we get into the species chapters. Of course, the use of strike indicators is a matter of personal choice. If you don't want to use a strike indicator, that's fine. However, don't let pressure from other anglers who "know better" be the determining factor as to whether or not you use these valuable tools.

A variety of strike indicators for warmwater fly fishing.

CLOTHING

The clothing that you wear when fly fishing warmwater lakes and streams will vary greatly through the seasons. In the summer you will likely be comfortable wet-wading in just shorts and wading shoes. As the weather cools off, you will probably want to put on waders to keep warm. Chest waders provide access to the most water, but hip waders are a cheaper alternative that can be packed along more easily.

A traditional fly-fishing vest is not necessary these days. Some warmwater anglers prefer to use chest packs, backpacks, or fanny packs to stow their gear. If you are going ultralight, a shirt with a couple of chest pockets will hold enough gear for a day of warmwater fly fishing.

Polarized sunglasses are essential. They will protect your eyes from the sun, not to mention errant casts. Polarized glasses also cut through the glare of the water's surface, allowing you to spot holding fish as well as structure and cover that you might miss without the aid of the glasses.

Regardless of the season, you will want to take along a comfortable hat when you go fly fishing. Whether you prefer full-brim hats or baseball caps, a hat will keep the sun out of your eyes and protect your head and ears from sunburn. A hat is also a handy place to stash fished flies so that they do not get your fly box wet.

ACCESSORIES

There are all sorts of accessories available for your fly-fishing pleasure. Some are necessary, while others are merely goofy gadgets. The list of indispensable items includes line nippers, a pocketknife, hemostats or needle-nose pliers, a hook hone, sunscreen, and insect repellant.

A net is optional for most warmwater fly fishing. You can easily land bass, panfish, and stripers by hand. Pike and muskellunge can be landed by hand, but it can be difficult to get a good hold on larger fish, not to mention that mouthful of razor-blade teeth! If you are going after big carp, you might want to pack a net or a Boga-Grip like saltwater anglers use. You don't have to worry about getting bitten by a carp, but they are tough fish and it's not easy to get a grip on a trophy-size one.

Useful accessories for warmwater fly fishing include fly floatant, hemostats, a multi-tool with pliers, a hook hone, and a pocketknife.

You should also consider how you will protect your gear. Investing in a hard-shelled tube for your fly rod (and actually keeping your rod in the tube) will ensure that you do not suffer a tragedy at the hands of a car door or trunk lid. If you are the type of angler who likes to run-and-gun from one fishing hole to another, you may wish to install a cartop carrier for your fly rods so that you do not have to break them down after every stop.

Nippers are essential for changing flies and cleaning up knots.
KYRA PERKINSON

Polarized sunglasses are essential for cutting glare on the water's surface and helping you locate fish.

BOATS

While far from necessary in most situations, a boat will certainly help you reach more water and more fish. Watercraft for warmwater fly fishing can range from simple canoes to loaded bass boats. You can even pack a float tube or "belly boat" into the backwoods for single-seat access to remote waters.

RECOMMENDED FLY-FISHING OUTFITS BY SPECIES

Largemouth Bass

A 9-foot, 8-weight fly rod with "bass bug" tapered line help you cast and fight largemouth bass. You may wish to step up to a 10-weight rig if you are fishing for lunker bass in heavy cover. Use tapered monofilament nylon leaders for top-water presentations and level fluorocarbon leaders for subsurface fishing.

Smallmouth Bass

A 9-foot, 6-weight rod with "bass bug" tapered line will handle most smallies. You can oversize the line by a size or two to make casting easier, especially on smaller streams. Use tapered monofilament nylon leaders for top-water and level fluorocarbon leaders for subsurface angling. A strike indicator will greatly improve your catch rate for stream-dwelling bronzebacks.

Panfish

A 4-weight rod between 7½ and 9 feet is great for panfish. Use a weight-forward fly line and a 5X tapered monofilament nylon leader.

Northern Pike and Muskellunge

An 8- to 10-weight rod between 9 and 10 feet will help you throw big flies at these fish all day. Overload your fly line by a size or two, and be sure to use a nylon-coated wire bite tippet.

Striped Bass

A 9-foot, 10-weight rod with an oversize "bass bug" tapered fly line will help you get big streamers in front of stripers. You may need to use a sinking head or a full-sink line when the fish are deep. A good disc-drag reel will help you land this hard-running fish.

White Bass

An 9-foot, 8-weight rod with "bass bug" tapered fly line is great for white bass. Use a tapered monofilament nylon leader for top-water presentations and a level fluorocarbon leader for subsurface fishing. Be sure to de-barb your hooks so that you don't waste time unhooking white bass in the middle of a feeding frenzy.

Carp

An 9-foot, 8- to 10-weight rod with a weight-forward fly line is tough enough for carp. Use 9- or 10-foot tapered monofilament nylon and fluorocarbon leaders, as carp are especially wary. You will want a good disc-drag fly reel when you hook into a carp.

CHAPTER 3

Basic Fly Casting and Line Control

There is no need to be intimidated by fly casting, even if you are completely new to the sport. Television sports programs, Internet fly-fishing forums, and angling literature are rife with dubious stories of pinpoint 100-foot casts. While there are certainly anglers who are capable of laying out 100 feet of line, these stories usually serve only to impress an audience while increasing the anxiety and self-doubt of new fly casters. In the real world, your ability to consistently place accurate 40- to 50-foot casts and the knowledge of how to control your line once it is on the water are far more important than making 100-foot casts.

Before we get into the specifics of casting, you should be aware of a couple of key points. Remember first that the fly line is weighted, not the fly or leader. The fly and the leader are essentially weightless, so the trick is to get the fly line moving in the direction that you want; the leader and fly will follow. This is exactly opposite from more familiar spinning and baitcasting tackle, so you will have to wrap your mind around a completely foreign concept if you are switching from spinning gear to fly tackle.

You should also remember that the fly rod is a casting tool. The motion of your fly line loads energy into the fly rod on your backcast, and that energy transfers into the line on the forward cast. Just like shooting free throws or throwing a shot put, technique wins out over raw power when you are fly casting. If you allow the rod to do the work for you, your casting and angling skills will improve. If you try to muscle the line out, your efforts will be met with poor presentations and a sore arm.

THE CLOCK FACE

In order to present the physical motions of an overhead cast, let's first assume that you are a right-handed caster. The technique is the same for left-handed anglers, but some of the references that I use will be opposite. Let's say that you are standing with your fly rod in your right hand, the rod tip pointing straight up. Imagine a large clock face off to your right side so that the rod tip is pointing to 12 o'clock. If you lower the rod tip straight in front of you, it is pointing at 9 o'clock. If you lower it straight behind you, it is pointing at 3 o'clock. We will use this imaginary clock face as a reference to the positions of your rod throughout the casting.

Keep in mind that the clock face, while a common analogy for fly-casting instruction, is just a learning tool. It is handy to remember the clock face as you are learning and practicing, but the clock face is really just a way for experienced casters to explain the basic motions of casting. As you gain experience and confidence, you will learn to cast by feel rather than the rigid numbers of the clock face.

1)

2)

3)

4)

To make a basic overhead cast: (1) Grip the rod handle with your thumb on top, keeping your wrist in line with your forearm. (2) Pick up the slack line from the water and accelerate the fly line behind you, stopping sharply at the 10 o'clock position so that the fly line straightens out behind you. (3) Accelerate forward, stopping sharply so that the fly line straightens out toward your target. (4) Lower the rod tip so that it is pointing toward the fly.

HOLDING THE FLY ROD

Hold the rod with your right hand on the grip, just above the reel. Grip the rod lightly and keep your thumb on top of the rod, pointing toward the rod tip. Your left hand will manage the fly line. Feed several feet of line out beyond the rod tip, then strip out a few more feet of line and gather it in your left hand. With a light grip on the rod grip, some line on the water (or on the lawn), and the slack line in your hand, you are ready to start casting.

The fly line will unroll in a loop toward your target as you cast forward. KYRA PERKINSON

Lower your arm to your side to make a sidearm cast. Watch the backcast to make sure that you don't get snagged.
KYRA PERKINSON

Pulling line down toward you with your left hand on the backcast and forward cast will "haul" the line, adding speed and distance to your cast. KYRA PERKINSON

THE OVERHEAD CAST

The overhead cast is the most basic fly cast. A mastery of this casting technique will open many doors, allowing you to learn other types of casts that can be used in special situations. You may even decide that the standard overhead cast is not the most effective way for you to present flies and abandon the technique altogether. Even so, learning the overhead cast is a solid introduction to the way that fly casting works.

Begin the overhead cast with your rod tip at 8 o'clock, as though you have just fished out a cast with no luck. The fly line is on the water in front of you, and you are ready to make another cast. If you rip the line off the water from this position, you will spook every fish in the stream. Instead, gather the slack line in your left hand and raise the rod tip smoothly until it is at about 10 o'clock. With the slack line in hand and the rod tip up, only the fly and some of the leader will be on the water. At this point you have "picked up" the line and can make your backcast without spooking the fish.

The backcast begins with your rod tip at 10 o'clock and the fly line picked up. Accelerate the rod tip over and behind your head, stopping at 2 o'clock. The motion should come from your elbow and shoulder, not from your wrist. It is critical that the acceleration is smooth and the stop is crisp, as this will throw the fly line behind you. Look over your right shoulder, and you will see the line unrolling in a loop. You should be conscious of how the rod feels in your hand. At the point that the loop unrolls, you will feel tension on the rod. This is the line loading the fly rod. Wait until the loop unrolls behind you so that the rod is fully loaded with energy. New fly casters often make a good initial backcast, but whip the line forward before the entire backcast has unrolled and loaded the rod. If your casts wind up as little piles of fly line 3 feet in front of you, it is very likely that you are beginning the forward cast before the rod has loaded.

The forward cast is the motion that will send the fly toward your target. At the end of the backcast, your rod tip will be at 2 o'clock. Accelerate the rod tip toward your target smoothly, and stop sharply at 10 o'clock. Give the rod a final snap with your wrist just before you stop, so that your thumb is pointing in the direction that you want your fly to go. This final snap will help punch the line toward your target. The most common mistake on the forward cast is to stop softly. Stopping sharply transfers the energy of the loaded rod back into the fly line. Stopping softly wastes casting energy and results in a weak forward cast.

When the forward cast is complete, your fly line will travel in a loop in front of you and unroll, just like it did on the backcast. As the loop unrolls, it will slow down your leader and fly so that you do not get a big splash when the fly lands. This loop is characteristic of good casting technique. The action of your fly rod and the weight of your line in comparison to the rod will determine how tight or open the loop is, but your casting technique is what actually forms the loop. If you find that your forward cast does not form a good loop, the first thing to check is your backcast. A poor backcast always leads to a weak forward cast. If your backcast is good but your forward cast is weak, be sure that you are stopping the forward cast sharply.

The forward cast stops at 10 o'clock, which is not the ideal angle for making most warmwater presentations. As the loop unrolls, gently lower your rod tip to 8 o'clock so that it is pointing toward your target. This will allow you to control the fly as it drops to the water and will put you in the perfect position to present your fly to the fish.

VARIATIONS ON THE OVERHEAD CAST

The particular conditions in which you are fishing will require different casting techniques. Throwing large bass bugs or weighted streamers is a very different game than casting dry trout flies. As you explore warmwater streams, you will encounter dense brush and tight casting quarters that make standard overhead casting very difficult. In addition, casting to pike, muskie, and striped bass will require a lot of long casts that would be difficult and tiring to achieve by simply casting overhead. There are a few special casting techniques that will help in such situations.

The Sidearm Cast

The sidearm cast is the simplest and most common variation of the overhead cast. To execute a sidearm cast, simply drop your casting arm to your side as you make the backcast and forward cast. This will lower the plane of your cast closer to the water. Other than being tilted closer to the water, the motion and physics of the sidearm cast are identical to the overhead cast.

The sidearm cast is useful when you need to cast beneath overhead brush and foliage. If you fish a lot of small streams, you will probably find that your casting begins to lean more toward a sidearm style. There is nothing wrong with that either. Both the overhead cast and the sidearm cast are efficient ways to put your flies in front of fish.

The Double Haul

The double haul can be tricky for both novice and experienced fly casters, but it is well worth the effort to learn this technique. The double haul is essentially an overhead cast with the addition of a "haul," or downward strip of the line, on both the backcast and the forward cast. This adds speed to the cast and allows you to cast more line with less effort.

Begin the double haul by making a standard backcast. As you raise the rod, pull the fly line down toward your belt with your left hand. When you stop the rod at the end of the backcast, the line that you have cast will continue backward. Feed the extra line that you hauled down back through the line guides, allowing the backcast to pull it backward. When the backcast has straightened out, accelerate the rod tip forward and strip the line down toward your belt again. Stop the rod tip sharply and feed the hauled line through the guides again. The momentum of the cast fly line will shoot the extra line that you hauled, allowing you to cast farther.

A good way to learn to double haul is to watch DVDs or online videos of great fly casters in action. When you watch Joan Wulff or Lefty Kreh cast, you will notice that they double haul on nearly every cast. They cast with such a cool, smooth technique that the double haul seems to be an unconscious part of their casting rhythm.

There is a lot going on when you double haul. The mechanics of the double haul can be confusing and you are likely to wind up with a few tangles as you learn, but don't be discouraged. Practice with slow, deliberate casting motions on the lawn until you can shoot a few feet of line. Once you become accustomed to the timing of the double haul, you can start to work on gaining more distance. Before you know it, you will have no problem dropping bass bugs on unsuspecting fish from 50 feet away.

The Roll Cast

The roll cast is another casting technique that can seem tricky at first. Unlike the other casts you have learned, the roll cast does not include a backcast. This is a handy trick when you are backed up against heavy brush and need to get your fly on the water.

To roll cast you need to leave some fly line on the water in front of you. Raise your rod so that the tip is pointing straight up. Let the line hang from your rod tip so that it forms a loose, open loop along the length of the rod. You need to have enough line out so that there is still some fly line on the water below this loop. Now accelerate in the direction you wish to cast and stop sharply, just like you are performing one-half of an overhead cast. The loop in the fly line will follow your rod tip and begin unrolling in the direction that you have cast.

Roll casting involves precise timing that is a bit confusing at first. Practice the basic motions of the roll cast on your lawn until you are comfortable with them. Take what you learn and try it out on the water before you actually use the roll cast for fish.

It can be difficult to pick up casting techniques from a book, and you will never become a proficient fly caster if you do not practice. Be sure to put in some time on your lawn, at the park, or from the bank of an open pond. If you have trouble, check out online videos of expert fly casters or look for an instructional video at the fly shop. Taking a lesson or two from a qualified casting instructor is the best way to learn proper casting techniques. For less than the cost of a new fly rod, an instructor will diagnose your casting, correct any problems, and offer the kind of advice that you simply cannot get from books.

A roll cast "unrolling" toward the target. Roll casting allows you to cast in tight quarters without having to backcast. KYRA PERKINSON

Keep your rod tip low and pointed toward the fly so that you can manipulate the fly at will or set the hook at a moment's notice. KYRA PERKINSON

Tuck the line between your forefinger or middle finger and the rod handle to keep it under control while presenting your fly. KYRA PERKINSON

LINE CONTROL AND FLY PRESENTATION

Casting is only one aspect of fly fishing. Unless you plan on join-
ing a professional fly-casting tour, the ability to throw a mile of line
doesn't mean much if you cannot control it on the water. The major
culprits that seek to steal control of your line are slack, drag, and a
poor rod angle.

Line Control on Still Water

Controlling your line on still water is largely a matter of keeping
slack line to a minimum. When your cast has landed on the water,
you should lower your rod so that the tip is pointing at the fly. Now
gather the slack line up in your left hand, and you have a tight-line
connection between your left hand and the fly. There should be no
slack hanging from the rod or any loops of line on the water. Your rod
tip is angled low, near the water, so that the rod does not flex when
you strip line. When you strip line with your left hand, the fly moves.
When a fish strikes, you can set the hook by stripping line and simultaneously raising the rod. Because there is no slack between your hand
and the fly, when you set the hook, the hook strikes the fish. As simple
as it seems, lowering your rod so that the tip is pointing at the fly and
gathering up slack line in your left hand are the key points to achiev-
ing perfect line control on still waters.

Line Control in Current

Controlling your fly line on moving water is a bit more challenging. The
current will always pull your line downstream and quickly whisk your
fly away from the targeted area. This is called "drag," and it can be used
to your advantage if you learn to control it.

The best way to make controlled presentations in current is to cast
at upstream and downstream angles rather than directly across the current. When you cast to a target straight across moving water, you are
immediately fighting the current. Your fly is likely to be dragged away
from the target before you can even attempt to correct the drift. Casting
upstream of your target will allow you to correct the drift by throwing

a little upstream slack into the line. This is called "mending" the line. Mending should be done in a controlled manner to achieve a desired result. Mending the line will allow your bass bug to drift into position before you begin your retrieve. Mending will also give subsurface flies a chance to sink deeper because the slack keeps the current from pulling your fly toward the surface.

Casting above your target at a downstream angle lets you swing the fly across the current. By varying your rod angle and feeding line into the drift, you can swing a streamer or bass bug downstream. You can also feed line directly downstream so that the current pulls your fly into a fallen tree or brushy cover that would be difficult to cast directly into.

Keep your rod tip close to the water and pointed toward your fly. Add slack sparingly so that you remain in control of the line and the fly. With a low rod angle and controlled amounts of slack in the line, you will be able to control your flies with line strips and rod-tip manipulation. Keeping a low rod angle will also allow plenty of room to raise your rod and set the hook when a fish strikes.

Bringing Your Fly to Life

Big warmwater gamefish like bass and pike go for big flies that mimic the action of familiar food sources. The action that you impart to your flies is a large part of warmwater fly-fishing success. You can impart action to your fly by stripping line or manipulating the line with your rod tip. Manipulating the fly with your rod tip has been condemned by some anglers because it introduces slack into the line, but cautious use of the technique adds wonderful, subtle action to your presentations. Keep your rod angle low, and be careful not to put too much slack line on the water.

As we move into the species chapters, we will have a closer look at line control and fly manipulation as they apply in different situations. Certain circumstances may require a little rule-bending, but you should never lose control of your line to the point that you cannot manipulate your fly or set the hook.

CATCHING FISH

Now let's get to the fun part: catching some fish! You have delivered a well-targeted cast and skillfully manipulated your fly right into the strike zone when . . . WHAM! There are a few things that you need to know to keep your fish hooked and bring it to hand.

Setting the Hook

When you are fishing with a tight line on still water, you can usually set the hook by simply stripping line with your left hand. A couple of good strikes like this will set the hook, then you can raise your rod to fight the fish.

Of course, raising your rod when a fish strikes is a natural reaction, but be sure that you are not counting on the rod to set the hook. By stripping line to set the hook, you do not lose energy when your rod flexes. The result is a more solid hook-set. You don't really need to worry about a bass leader breaking like a trout leader, and there is no slack line to pick up before the hook sets. Of course, keeping a low rod angle during the excitement of a strike can be difficult, but be sure to give the line a good strip-strike or two so that you are hooked up tight.

Warmwater fly fishing on creeks and rivers will usually involve a controlled amount of slack line on the water. When a fish takes your fly in moving water, it is best to raise the rod and strip line simultaneously in order to pick up the slack and get a good hook-set.

Fighting Fish

Landing a fish on fly gear is not the same as landing fish with spinning or bait-casting gear. You must use the reel to recover line with spinning and bait-casting gear, but fly line can easily be retrieved on the reel or by hand. Depending on your gear, the particular situation, and the species you are hooked into, you may wish to simply land the fish "off the reel" or try to get it "on the reel."

Warmwater fish like bass, panfish, and smaller pike will put up a tough fight, but they do not run far. It is reasonable to expect that you can bring these fish to hand without actually getting them on the reel. In fact, trying to get a fish on the reel that you could have landed without doing so can cost you the fish. Giving any slack to a fish opens the door for the fish to throw your hook. If you are focused on getting the fish on the reel, you run the risk of letting slack develop and getting thrown.

Long-running warmwater fish like striped bass and carp almost always require that you get the fish on the reel. A quality disc-drag reel will put extra pressure on these fish and prevent your line from becoming a tangled mess when the fish runs. If a fish runs straight at you, it might be necessary to strip the line quickly in order to keep a tight connection with the fish. You can also land some running species off the reel if you hook the fish close to your own position. In this situation it is much easier to pull in 10 feet of line by hand than to recover 50 feet of stripped line from the ground or the boat deck in order to get the fish on the reel.

Your fly rod plays an important part in landing fish as well. As the rod flexes, it absorbs some of the shock from your terminal tackle. If you eliminate the rod from the fight by keeping the tip pointed at the fish, you are simply asking for the hook, the leader, or a knot to fail.

You can also use the rod to tire fish and to steer them out of snags and cover. Fighting a fish with a high rod angle will force the fish closer to the surface and keep it out of cover. Angling the rod away from a running fish lets the rod flex deeply and will help you tire the fish more quickly. A very low rod angle can force the fish's head down, which will often subdue a stubborn fish.

CHAPTER 4

Structure and Cover

Just like coldwater and saltwater species, warmwater gamefish have different needs depending on species, environmental conditions, and the time of year. Meeting the basic requirements of food, shelter, reproduction, and suitable water temperature encompasses most of the everyday lives of gamefish, and these needs vary across the range of fish species. Knowing the requirements of the fish you seek will help you determine the best waters in which to catch them. Fly fishing for warmwater species often involves blind casting, or "searching" out areas that are likely to be inhabited by fish. Many of the basic requirements needed for fish to survive are related to structure and cover. Understanding these basic concepts will put you on fish more often than not.

STRUCTURE

Structure is a natural or man-made feature that alters the underwater topography of a lake, river, or creek. Examples of structure can include natural features like underwater ridges, drop-offs, and glacial gouges in the lake bottom. Man-made structure can include submerged ditches, buildings, and road beds that are permanently flooded beneath a reservoir.

Many warmwater gamefish relate to structure and cover. Do you see the bass hiding among these rocks?

Warmwater gamefish like bass relate to structure in the same way that we relate to streets and roads. Following the contours of structure allows gamefish to stay oriented as they move through the water. Although the movement of warmwater gamefish may seem random, it is actually driven by the needs for food, shelter, favorable water temperature, and reproduction. Fish move from place to place as conditions change, and the structure of the bottom is the highway that they use.

Though fish regularly travel along the contours of bottom structure, there may be underlying reasons why gamefish are found in relation to structure. The structure may attract baitfish seeking shelter from predation by gamefish like bass and pike. In turn, the presence of baitfish attracts predators. In this case the structure not only concentrates prey species, but also makes an ideal killing field for the predators. Structure provides an ambush point for predatory fish, which can hide directly behind a structural feature in much the same way that a hunter can remain undetected by deer in an adjacent valley.

Sometimes structure is not the direct reason that gamefish are present. Structure may simply delineate a desirable area from one that is not so favorable for gamefish. For example, the shallow water along a submerged point will warm early in the spring, attracting baitfish and gamefish with ideal water temperatures. The structure is visible and easily discerned by experienced anglers as a hot spot, but the favorable water temperature is the environmental factor that actually attracts the fish.

In lakes and ponds, look for areas where shallow water drops off to deeper water. These areas provide gamefish plenty of forage in the shallows with the nearby shelter of deep water. Features like submerged points, rock piles, and mid-water reefs are excellent areas to pick up bass and panfish with a fly.

Examples of structure in reservoirs can vary greatly depending on the reservoir's depth, the type of terrain that was flooded, and how much variation in water level the reservoir experiences. Former hills become underwater bumps, ridges become submerged points, and low areas become deep holes. Man-made structures such as fence rows, roads, and even buildings are often flooded when a reservoir is filled. These features can become a permanent part of the underwater landscape, creating man-made structure that attracts baitfish and gamefish.

Structure can be identified on detailed maps of lakes and reservoirs. Many of these popular publications specifically depict underwater structure, and a basic knowledge of reading contour lines will identify other prime spots. You should pick up a map of any large lake that you are going to fish so that you can narrow down the areas that are most likely to hold fish. A depth-finder is another valuable tool for locating structure in unfamiliar water. I am not a big fan of electronic fish-finders, but I hold no grudge against anglers who choose to use them. They will certainly help you locate underwater structure and fish on a large body of water.

Structure can be more easily discerned in creeks and rivers. The current will indicate the type of bottom in a particular stretch of water. Structure in moving water includes deep holes, drop-offs, ledges, and rocky riffles. All of these examples affect how the water flows, making identification easier than in still water. Structure in moving water provides gamefish relief from the current and concentrates baitfish and other food sources as well. Rocky riffles are breeding grounds for many aquatic insects and microscopic invertebrates that baitfish feed on. Rocky ledges are prime hiding spots for crayfish, which are a favorite food of bass. The structure indirectly attracts gamefish by concentrating choice prey species.

Although the specific type of structure may vary from one body of water to the next, you should approach any type of water with the common elements of structure in mind. On large bodies of water like lakes and reservoirs, identifying structure will help you narrow down vast expanses of water to a few likely areas. In moving water, a thorough understanding of how structure affects the flow will help you dial in the best holding water. Regardless of where you fish, identifying structure and putting your fly on it will lead to more hook-ups.

COVER

Paradoxically, cover is essentially any place that provides fish protection from predators or a place from which predatory fish can ambush their prey. Aquatic vegetation, fallen trees, and flooded timber are prime examples of cover. Unlike structure, which is strictly defined as a bottom feature, cover can occur at any level of the water column. In fact, objects outside the water such as docks, overhead trees, and even the shade can be considered cover.

While cover provides gamefish protection from predators, it also concentrates prey species seeking shelter. The numbers of prey species such as minnows, crayfish, and insect larvae in and around cover also attracts gamefish like bass and pike. Aside from open-water predators like stripers and white bass, all warmwater gamefish relate to cover at some time. Identification of cover is essential to warmwater fly-fishing success. Luckily, cover is often much easier to identify than structure.

In fertile lakes and ponds, cover is likely to consist of some sort of vegetation. Aquatic plants like hydrilla and water lily are great spots for warmwater gamefish. You should also look for any trees that have fallen into the water. The branches create a breeding ground for the aquatic invertebrates that baitfish and small panfish feed on. This concentration of baitfish attracts gamefish. In addition, the fallen tree provides cover for the gamefish from the predators that feed on them, such as eagles and otters. Natural lakes and well-established man-made impoundments are often lined with trees and overhanging foliage. Be sure to look for fallen timber, and concentrate your presentations on these key pieces of cover.

Fishing cover with a fly rod on a larger reservoir usually means sticking to the water's edge. The middle of a large reservoir can be productive if you can identify and reach bottom structure, but the bottom of a reservoir is often out of reach of fly anglers. The edges of a reservoir, however, offer a great variety of cover. Creek arms and back bays offer plenty of overhanging vegetation. If your favorite reservoir enjoys a fairly consistent water level, these quiet corners can be a great place to find aquatic vegetation as well. If the water level of your reservoir fluctuates, don't despair. Low water levels will reveal hidden cover such as flooded timber or man-made structures that were once on dry ground. Reservoirs that are frequently drawn down often feature standing flooded timber, which is prime cover for warmwater species like panfish and crappies. You shouldn't overlook man-made cover like docks, riprap dams, and even the weedy edges of a swimming beach. Warmwater gamefish will flock to any type of cover that meets the basic needs of food, shelter, reproduction, and favorable water conditions.

Cover plays an important part in the location of stream-dwelling warmwater gamefish as well. In addition to aquatic vegetation and overhanging foliage, look for rocky outcroppings and undercut banks on moving water. Limestone streams offer especially good fishing, as these streams are usually very fertile and offer lots of rocky cover.

Structure and cover are important concepts, and your ability to identify them will greatly increase your warmwater fly-fishing success. That said, I encourage you to become adept at identification of structure and cover, but don't get hung up on strict definitions. Warmwater game-fish often behave in ways that we do not understand. A tempting piece of cover may be empty because the water is too cold, while an adjacent patch of "dead water" holds fish because of an unseen submerged weed bed. In the end, it does not matter whether a particular lie is defined as structure or cover, only that it holds fish. Focus your efforts on what you can see and identify, and you will catch fish.

These are but a few examples of the types of structure and cover that attract gamefish. We will have a closer look at structure and cover as they relate to specific fish in the species chapters.

CHAPTER 5

Fly Fishing for Bass

There are many reasons for the enormous popularity of bass fishing across North America. Largemouth and smallmouth bass are widely distributed from coast to coast. They eagerly take flies, put up tenacious fights, and reach trophy size in waters that are accessible to the everyday angler.

Largemouth bass and smallmouth bass may be found in the same body of water, though waters in which largemouth bass are the dominant species rarely hold smallmouth bass in any numbers. Don't fall for the common misconception that smallmouth bass are "cool-water" fish, thriving only in waters that fall somewhere between the temperature ranges of a trout stream and a bass pond. In fact, largemouth and smallmouth bass are both sluggish when water temperatures are cool, and both species become more active as water temperatures rise. The geographic area in which you are fishing, the type of structure and cover, and the average water clarity are better indicators of the type of bass that live in a given body of water than the water temperature.

I have caught plenty of smallmouth bass in murky farmland streams from which I expected only largemouth bass. I have also hooked largemouth bass in cool, crystalline headwaters that appeared to be perfect smallmouth water. A favorite smallmouth stream in west-central

Indiana once surprised me with an 18-inch largemouth that took a size 6 Woolly Bugger. I read in the paper several years later that a fellow angler caught a big tiger muskellunge from that same stream. Apparently the muskie had escaped from a reservoir during a flood and had survived in that little stream for a few years before it fell for his Rapala. The point here is that you can't be sure what type of bass, or any other gamefish for that matter, live in your local water unless you get out there and fish it.

Fortunately, there is no real difference between fly fishing for largemouth and smallmouth bass, aside from distinguishing the type of structure and cover favored by either species. Both species will hit the same flies when presented properly. There are a few special situations that call for particular flies or methods that work best for one species or the other, but you will do better to identify the type of cover and structure that you are fishing rather than worrying about whether your flies are for largemouth or smallmouth.

With that in mind, let's look at some proven methods for catching bass in various types of water. Most of these techniques will produce both largemouth and smallmouth bass, depending on the species that is present where you are fishing. Pay close attention to the type of water, the direction in which you are fishing, and the types of structure and cover associated with these techniques. If you master these techniques and sharpen your ability to read the water, you will catch plenty of bass.

LAKES AND RESERVOIRS

The smashing strike of a bass inhaling your top-water bug is one of the most exciting moments in fly fishing. This method is favored by many fly anglers, not only because of its effectiveness, but also because it is fun to see the take on top.

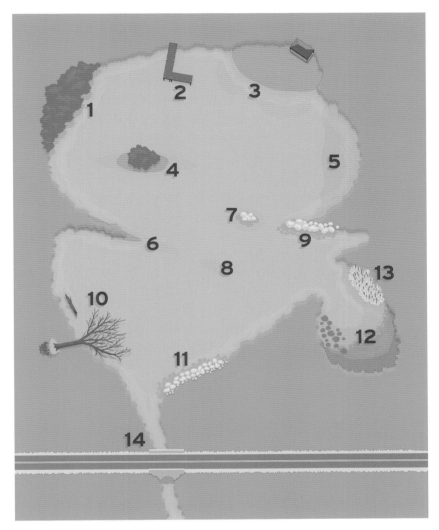

Where to fly fish for bass in lakes:

1. Overhanging brush
2. Docks and piers
3. Swimming beach
4. Mid-lake island and nearby shallow water
5. Shallow shoreline with steep drop-off
6. Point (smallmouth hot spot)
7. Mid-lake rock pile (smallmouth hot spot)
8. Hump or saddle (smallmouth hot spot)
9. Rocky point (smallmouth hot spot)
10. Fallen timber and sunken logs
11. Riprap-lined bank (smallmouth hot spot)
12. Shallow cove with lily pads and vegetation
13. Reeds and cattails
14. Bridge

Bass Bugs

The Two-Cast Presentation

If you are in position to make a cast perpendicular to an edge, a piece of cover, or a specific target, throw your fly right on top of the target and make a presentation, then make another cast well beyond the target and present your bass bug again. The first cast puts your bug in the prime spot, while the second cast will swim your fly right through the sweet spot in addition to making a presentation to fish that are holding beyond the target area. If you made the long cast first, you would run the risk of spooking fish in the target area with your fly line.

Pounding the Banks

If you are fishing from a boat, one of the best ways to fish bass bugs is to pound the bank. Both largemouth and smallmouth bass will hang out around bank-side features like fallen trees, overhanging foliage, docks, weed beds, sea walls, and riprap. You simply need to get your boat close enough that you can make accurate casts and start laying your bass bug in close to the cover. This is much easier if you are fishing with a partner so that one of you can keep the boat in position while the other fishes. Be sure to take turns; a good rule is that one angler fishes until he or she either lands a bass or misses a strike, then it is the other angler's turn. There are no referees on the water, so I'll leave it up to you to decide what counts as a strike. This makes for a nice air of competition and provides both anglers plenty of shots at good bass cover.

Fishing the banks of a lake or pond allows you the luxury of making a slow presentation. Identify your target area and make an accurate cast. Bass bugs land with a nice plop, and that's fine. Let the rings die down while you get into position, then strip your line so that the bug pops or dives. Retrieve your bass bug as slowly as you can tolerate, and be ready to set the hook even when your fly is at rest. Regardless of how tempting a bit of cover is, you don't need to hit one spot a dozen times; two or three good presentations to a piece of cover will most likely draw a strike if there is going to be one.

Target Shooting on Lakes and Ponds

Lake and pond banks are not the only place you can catch top-water bass. Bass frequently hold around submerged timber, stumps, and weed beds in bays and mid-lake shallows. Using the same boat technique, cast as close to the cover as you can. If you hit a stump with your bass bug, that's great. Make a few slow presentations to the target from different angles using the two-cast presentation. Change up the cadence of your retrieve by alternating long and short line strips with varied pauses between. It is hard to say which side of an open-water target bass will prefer, so if you can hit every likely target from more than one side, you will increase your hookups.

Bass Bugging on the Edge

Bass frequently hold around areas where an edge is formed. Examples of edges in a lake can include a shallow area that drops off into deep

A fine example of a Lake Lanier spotted bass.
HENRY COWEN

water, a sandy bottom surrounded by thick weeds, a smooth bottom with piles of riprap or natural rocks, and a natural or man-made reef surrounded by deep water. You can find edges along the banks of a lake as well as in the middle of the water. Hidden edges like mid-lake reefs or shallows can be especially productive because most bass anglers pound the shoreline while ignoring less-obvious cover in open water.

You can present a bass bug either parallel or perpendicular to the edge. Say you have located a nice rocky edge that falls off into deep water. If you are set up to cast along the length of the edge, lay out a long cast parallel to the edge and make your presentation along the length. You can make a few casts farther up the edge as well as a few over the deeper water to be sure that you are putting your fly over fish that may be holding shallower or deeper.

You can also fish edges by making a right-angle presentation. Set up so that you can cast perpendicular to the length of the edge and make a two-cast presentation. Move along quickly as you work edges at a right angle. Two casts without a strike is enough, then move a few feet and try again so that you don't hang around the same spot too long.

Bass Bugs for Still Waters

You should carry an assortment of sliders, divers, and poppers when bass bugging still water. Pack along bass bugs in hook sizes 4 through 2/0, but be aware that the overall size of your fly, not the hook size, is the most critical aspect. Your bass bugs should range from 1 inch in length for still, clear water up to 6 inches long for murky water, wind-rippled waters, and giant bass.

Equipment for Still-Water Bass Bugging

An 8-weight, 9-foot moderate-fast to fast-action graphite fly rod is great for throwing big bass bugs on open water. Oversize your fly line by one or two line-weights to make casting easier. Use knotless tapered monofilament leaders between 6 and 9 feet long so that the leader does not pick up algae or weeds. Manufactured knotless tapered leaders that are rated for bass have heavier butt sections that will help your cast turn over.

Swimming Streamers in Lakes and Reservoirs

You can effectively imitate baitfish using non-weighted or lightly weighted swimming streamers in lakes. This technique allows you the versatility of searching shallow waters with your fly and quickly making a precise presentation if you spot a cruising bass.

Target Shooting with Swimming Streamers

Look for cover and structure that are likely to hold bass, and make an accurate cast to the target. Depending on the depth that you wish to present your fly, you can wait a moment or two for the fly to sink. Don't be taken by surprise if a bass snatches your fly while it is sinking. The fluttering action of long-winged streamer patterns as they sink is very enticing. If you do not get a strike, begin retrieving your fly with a varied series of line strips. Make short strips and long strips with random pauses so that your streamer swims like a crippled baitfish. Be sure that you fish out the target area, but leave enough line on the water so that you can pick up and make another cast quickly, because target shooting is most effective when you make a lot of precision presentations.

Bass have small, harmless teeth.

Pounding the Bank with Swimming Streamers

You can make quick work of searching a bank with a swimming streamer by slowly paddling or trolling parallel to the shore. Maintain a comfortable casting distance from the bank and cast right up to the water's edge. Make a few strips to swim your streamer out over deeper water, then pick up and cast again. A majority of bank-side strikes will occur from the moment your fly hits the water until you have made five or six strips, so move quickly and cover the water. Swimming streamers have the best action when they are stripped through open water, so rapidly retrieve your fly toward deeper water. You can make slow bank-side presentations with a bass bug, but strip swimming streamers quickly to draw strikes.

Swimming Streamers over Structure and Cover

Swimming streamers are particularly effective for fishing over submerged cover or structure. This is a great technique for a piece of cover like a completely submerged log or some structure such as a rocky underwater ridge. Select a target area and cast your streamer right on the bull's-eye. Cover the target area using the two-cast presentation. Divide the feature into sections and repeat the two-cast technique until you have thoroughly fished it out.

Swimming streamers can also be used to make subtle presentations to rocky submerged points in reservoirs. These are the points that were once ridges above the surface, but are now flooded and descend slowly into the depths. Position your boat parallel to the length of the ridge and cast your fly onto the shallowest part of the ridge. Strip your streamer slowly, with long pauses, so that it sinks a little deeper each time you pause. This will make the streamer descend the face of the ridge in a stair-step fashion, just like gear anglers do with blade baits and spinning lures.

Swimming Streamers for Still Waters

It is important that your swimming streamers have good action, but there is little weight to add action to these flies. You cannot count on the current to impart action on still water, so I like to use streamers tied on short-shank "saltwater" hooks. Swimming streamers with long wings and body materials that extend well past the hook shank have more action than traditional streamers tied on long-shank streamer hooks. Lefty's Deceiver is a great example of a short-shank streamer that has a lot of action, and it is my go-to swimming streamer pattern. Dave Whitlock's Hare Worm and John Barr's Bouface streamer are always good choices as well. You can modify popular bucktail and streamer patterns into short-shank swimming streamers by tying the body of the pattern as an underwing of Flashabou or Krystal Flash rather than lashing the body to the hook shank.

Equipment for Still-Water Swimming Streamers

An 8-weight, 9-foot graphite rod will easily cast light swimming streamers. Present non-weighted swimming streamers with a floating weight-forward fly line and a 6- to 9-foot knotless tapered monofilament leader. This will allow lighter streamers to turn over and will keep the streamer closer to the surface. If you are fishing lightly weighted swimming streamers into deeper water, you can switch to a level fluorocarbon leader, which

Gripping a bass by the lower lip will keep it calm while you unhook it.

71

will turn over with the heavier fly and will not impede the streamer from sinking. Consider placing a strike indicator at the line-to-leader connection if you are fishing swimming streamers deep.

Bottom Streamers in Lakes and Reservoirs

Top-water and swimming streamers are great fun because you usually see the strike. As you spend time on the water, however, you will learn that a lot of fish are taken on the bottom. Use these bottom-streamer techniques to hook up bass when they are deep.

Bottom Streamers on the Edge

Crayfish, madtoms, and sculpins can be found in heavy cover and become vulnerable to predation when they venture out into the open. This is why bass like to hang around edges. You can fish an edge with a bottom streamer by casting along its length or perpendicular to it. Bottom streamers will sink quickly in the absence of a current, so let your fly hit the bottom and retrieve it with short line strips and rod-tip manipulation. This will create a tempting jig-like action that attracts bass that are lurking in nearby cover. Whether you make your presentation parallel or perpendicular to the edge, be sure that you are fishing along the clean side of the edge. Casting into heavy weeds, submerged timber, or rock piles with a bottom streamer is a guaranteed way to get snagged. Put your streamer on the edge, and use action to lure the bass out.

The Deep-Water Retrieve

I think that the practical depth limits of fly-fishing tackle is around 15 or 20 feet, though it is possible to get flies much deeper. You can search the bottom of a lake or reservoir with a bottom streamer just like you would with a heavy spinning jig. Rather than blind casting, however, try to identify some sort of structure that bass would relate to. Consider the edge where a shallow bay or ridge drops off into deeper water. Features like these often hold bass at a specific level depending on the season, the water temperature, and the light.

Cast a bottom streamer into the shallowest part of the feature so that it immediately hits bottom. Retrieve it with line strips and rod-tip manipulation so that the streamer hops along the bottom, slowly going deeper and deeper. This is a similar technique to the stair-step technique used with swimming streamers, but you allow your bottom streamer to hit bottom on every hop. The result looks a lot like a crayfish or some tasty critter heading for deeper water. Make this presentation carefully and patiently. If there are bass holding on the structure you are fishing, you will eventually get down to their level, and they aren't likely to ignore any mouthful-size passersby.

Fishing Bottom Streamers from the Bank

Up to this point we have not really covered any techniques that are specifically geared toward bank anglers. Of course, you can use any of these still-water techniques on foot if you can find the right place to make a presentation. However, reversing the deep-water retrieve is probably the best way to hook up bass from shore.

Another monster Michigan largemouth landed and released. CHAD RAICH

Use this technique from an area where the shore or an easily waded shallow drops off into deep water. I wouldn't advise wading onto a submerged ridge for safety's sake, but if you can wade out onto a shallow shelf or locate a bank that drops off quickly, you can catch plenty of bass from shore. Cast your bottom streamer out into the deep water and allow enough time for it to sink to the bottom. A bright strike indicator will help you pick up subtle takes. Retrieve your fly with short line strips and rod-tip raises just like you did when fishing bottom streamers from shallow to deep water. Now you have a bite-size morsel climbing out of the depths, right past hungry bass. This is a great way to hook up a few bass when you don't have a boat, and it is a lot more effective than blind casting because it presents the fly at many different depths.

Bottom Streamers for Still Waters

Lead-wire wraps will sink a fly, but you will get much better action out of your bottom streamers if you place the weight off-center. Using beads or dumbbell eyes is the best way to get offset weight on streamers. Big bottom streamers like heavily weighted Clouser Minnows and Half-and-Half flies are sure to get the attention of lurking bass. In shallower water you can use bead-head patterns like Woolly Buggers or a Clouser Minnow tied with bead-chain eyes. The offset weight of patterns like these produces an up-and-down action that is similar to the jigs used by bait-casting anglers and is much more effective than simply adding lead-wire wraps to standard streamer patterns.

Equipment for Still-Water Bottom Streamers

Use an 8- or 9-weight, 9-foot graphite rod with an oversize weight-forward floating line to present bottom streamers to moderate depths. You can use a sinking line to get more depth, but do not oversize a sinking line because it will be too heavy for your fly rod. An 8- to 14-pound-test level fluorocarbon leader will present your bottom streamers nicely. Use a 6-foot leader for relatively shallow presentations and leaders up to 12 feet for more depth penetration. Attaching a small strike indicator at the line-to-leader connection will greatly improve your hookup rate.

CREEKS AND RIVERS

For many anglers, moving water is the greatest venue for top-water fly fishing. The sound of flowing water, the surrounding scenery, and the unabashed fury of a hooked river bass make streams the top choice for many top-water bass anglers.

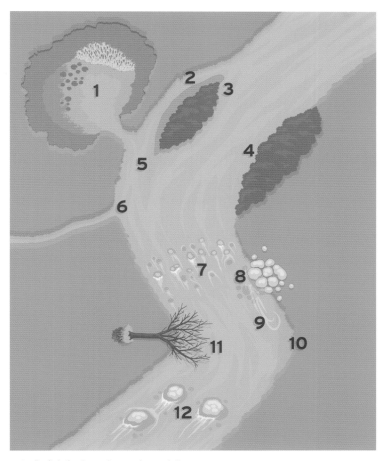

Where to fly fish for bass in creeks and rivers:

1. Swampy backwater (largemouth hot spot)
2. Side channel
3. Island with brushy cover
4. Overhanging brush
5. Shallow point off midstream island
6. Feeder stream
7. Riffles (smallmouth hot spot)
8. Rocky outcropping (smallmouth hot spot)
9. Current eddy
10. Deep outside bend
11. Fallen timber
12. Boulders (pocket water)

Bass Bugs

Target Shooting Bass Bugs in Rivers and Creeks

You can select likely targets and present bass bugs to them on rivers and creeks, just like you can on still water. The difference is that the current will inevitably drag your bass bug downstream. Because of this, when you are target shooting on moving water, you will have to initiate your retrieve sooner than you would on still water. Identify your target and cast as close as possible, then make your presentation with long and short strips and pauses. Depending on the speed of the current, you may only get a few strips before your bass bug is out of the target zone, so accurate casting is a must.

Across-and-Downstream Bass Bugging

If you want to fish cover that is too difficult to cast into, you can use the current to your advantage by letting your bass bug drift into position before retrieving. Say you want to fish the water directly beneath some overhanging foliage that lies at a downstream angle on the opposite bank. Casting directly into the cover will probably cost you a fly, but you can get in there by casting across stream and allowing the current to carry your bass bug into the heart of the cover. You may have to throw a mend or two into the drift so that your bass bug winds up where you want it, but there is no need to go for a drag-free dry-fly drift. Just let the current drag your bass bug where you want it, then begin your retrieve.

Downstream Bass Bugging

Of course, you can carry this to the extreme by casting your bass bug at a downstream angle or even directly downstream. This would be a serious faux pas in trout angling, but can have wonderful results for bass buggers. Bass bugs do not really resemble anything in particular. At the risk of anthropomorphizing our finny friends, bass most likely take topwater bass bugs out of curiosity as much as for any other reason. If you cannot seem to keep your bass bug in front of fish long enough to draw a strike, try casting the fly downstream. You will be able to hold the bass bug in place, retrieve it upstream, and allow it to drift downstream. In

Leaving bass in the water when you unhook them is the best way to ensure a successful release.

addition, the current will enhance the bass bug's action. It sometimes takes a minute or two to get the attention of a wary bass, so don't be afraid to let your bass bug hang downstream.

Bass Bugs for Moving Waters

You should carry sliders, divers, and poppers in a wide range of sizes for bass bugging on rivers and creeks. Water clarity, depth, current speed, and the smoothness of the surface will all play key roles in deciding which flies work best. Ultra-clear water with high visibility may require a size 6 slider to get any takes. On the other hand, you might need a 6-inch-long Dahlberg Diver to get the bass's attention on a big river with high, murky water. Water conditions can change in a hurry, especially if you fish tailwaters where flows can vary dramatically from one hour to the next. The best way to be prepared for any water condition is to keep a well-stocked box of bass bugs.

Equipment for Bass Bugging on Creeks and Rivers

Take into account the size of water you are fishing and how much room you will have to cast. On a big, wide-open river, you can use an 8-weight, 9-foot fast-action graphite rod to deliver your bass bugs. Creeks and smaller rivers that are choked with overhead foliage will either require a shorter fly rod or special casting techniques, such as roll-casting and sidearm casting. Manufactured knotless tapered monofilament leaders between 6 and 9 feet long are great for bass bugging on streams.

Swimming Streamers

Swimming streamers imitate baitfish and can be very effective for bass in rivers and creeks. You are not limited to the traditional "wet-fly swing" when presenting these versatile flies, however.

Swimming Streamers in Slack Water

Many rivers and creeks feature areas of slack water. These could be sloughs, backwaters, swamps, or simply flat areas where the flow spreads out and slows down. The lack of current allows aquatic plant growth, which attracts baitfish and bass. You can present swimming streamers in slack water by using the two-cast presentation. Divide areas of slack water into sections and cover the water thoroughly. If you are fishing over aquatic vegetation, be sure to keep your swimming streamer moving so that you do not get hung up.

Eddies and current seams can create slack water as well. Look for whirlpools, foam lines, and slick spots in the current. These all indicate a seam in the current that could hold bass. Cast swimming streamers above a current seam or eddy so that the streamer drifts naturally into the slack water, then animate your streamer with line strips and rod-tip manipulation to give the impression of a struggling or crippled minnow.

The Wet-Fly Swing for Streamers

The wet-fly swing is a traditional technique used to present wet flies to downstream trout. You can use a modified version of the technique to catch bass in rivers and creeks. Identify likely cover or structure and position yourself upstream and slightly across from the target. Cast across the current and slightly downstream, which should still be above your targeted area. Follow the drift of your streamer with your rod tip, manipulating the line with the rod tip and by tightening up or feeding more slack into the drift. This will cause your streamer to rise and fall in the current. As the streamer drifts directly downstream, your line will tighten up. If you have planned your drift well, this should put the fly right in your original targeted area. Not only have you presented the streamer to any fish that were holding above your target, but you now have the streamer hanging in a prime spot where you can make it swim by raising and lowering the rod tip and stripping or feeding line.

The Swimming Streamer Strip-and-Flip

You can easily present swimming streamers to tough downstream targets using the strip-and-flip method. Position yourself well above a snag-filled target such as a fallen tree. Cast or swing a swimming streamer so that it drifts right up to the target. Hold the streamer on a tight line so that it hangs alluringly just above the cover. You can manipulate the streamer with your rod tip so that it rises and falls in the current. After a minute or so, retrieve the streamer with several line strips, then flip the line to your left or right a bit and reposition the rod tip so that the streamer drifts back into another part of the cover. You can use the strip-and-flip over and over to make multiple presentations with one cast.

Swimming Streamers for Moving Water

Non-weighted streamers such as traditional bucktails and feather-wing patterns will swim in current if they are cast far enough above a target to allow them to sink. You can encourage non-weighted streamers to sink by feeding slack line into the drift. In swift current or when casting downstream, you will need to add a bit of weight to your patterns. Streamers with off-center weight like Clouser Minnows and Bead-Head Woolly Buggers have fish-attracting jigging action. Carry streamers in various lengths from 2 to 6 inches so that you will have all water conditions covered.

Equipment for Swimming Streamers on Creeks and Rivers

Present swimming streamers with a 6- to 8-weight, 9-foot rod if possible. The long rod will help you control the line and your streamers. Use a 6- to 9-foot-long knotless tapered monofilament leader for presenting swimming streamers near the surface. You may prefer a level fluorocarbon leader between 8- and 14-pound test for deeper presentations. Use a strike indicator at the line-to-leader connection if you cannot see your streamer as you are presenting it.

Bottom Streamers

Bass are frequently found at or near the bottom of creeks and rivers. They hold there for protection from overhead predators, to escape the perpetual current, and for more favorable water temperatures. Use heavily weighted bottom streamers to break through the current and hook up with bottom-hugging hogs.

Searching Pools with Bottom Streamers

It is well worth the effort to search out deep pools with a bottom streamer, especially when bass may be driven deeper due to cool weather or bright sunlight. Position yourself at the bottom of a pool and work your way toward the head so that you do not spook fish by kicking up silt with your presentation. Working perpendicular to the length of the pool, use the two-cast presentation to search the middle of the pool, then cast across the pool and search along the same line. Retrieve your bottom streamer directly across the pool using line strips of various lengths, random pauses, and rod-tip manipulation. Once you have fished your streamer through the pool, take a few steps upstream and repeat the process. Use a strike indicator at the line-to-leader connection to help you pick up light strikes.

Target Shooting with Bottom Streamers

Don't be too quick to pass over areas that lack cover on a bass stream. There may be bass holding deeper on bottom structure like rocky ledges or submerged boulders. Polarized sunglasses will help you pick out structure like this, and once you have identified the feature, you need to get your fly on it. Fish bottom structure by casting across the current with a heavily weighted bottom streamer that will get down quickly. If your streamer is too light, it will be swept out of the target zone, so don't be shy about tossing some lead. Use the two-cast presentation, dropping your streamer right on the target, followed by a longer cast worked through the target area. Work the feature from both the upstream and downstream sides, and then move on to the next target.

The Upstream Streamer Presentation and the "Holschlag Crayfish Hop"

There are situations when casting upstream is your best option to make a good presentation to bass. Of course, casting upstream means that your fly will immediately be swept back toward you, introducing all sorts of slack and preventing the fly from getting down to the bottom. Presenting a bottom streamer that carries enough weight to cut through the current will eliminate much of the difficulties when casting upstream. You must still strip line to keep up with the drift. A bottom streamer will stick to the bottom and out of the swiftest current, slowing the fly's drift and keeping it in the target zone longer.

For years I fished heavily weighted bottom streamers upstream for bass with a fair amount of success. I used a short, knotless, tapered leader for shallow water and a short, level length of fluorocarbon for deeper water. But smallmouth bass guide and author Tim Holschlag's book *Smallmouth Fly Fishing* permanently changed my mind as far as upstream streamer presentations are concerned. His "Crayfish Hop" technique involves casting a bottom streamer upstream on a long leader with a strike indicator attached at the line-to-leader connection. The long leader allows your streamer to get down better, and the strike indicator greatly increases your ability to detect light takes.

This smallmouth bass fell for a Holschlag Hackle Fly presented with the "Crayfish Hop" technique.

The Pocket-Water Method with Bottom Streamers, or the "Modified Brooks Method"

While we are on the topic of other anglers' signature techniques, I would like to share with you a modified version of the "Brooks Method" that works great for bass in boulder-strewn pocket water. Charles Brooks was a Western trout angler who developed a short-line method of fishing swift pocket water with heavy nymphs to catch big trout. I first read about the method in his book *Nymph Fishing for Larger Trout*. In swift pocket water where smallmouth bass live, you can use this modified version to hook up bottom-hugging bass.

Use a 4- to 5-foot-long level fluorocarbon leader and a heavily weighted bottom streamer like a Bead-Head Woolly Bugger, a

Holschlag Hackle Fly, or a Clouser Minnow. Make a short cast into the deep pocket water around a midstream boulder and follow the streamer's drift with your rod tip, keeping the tip high and the line tight. You don't need to manipulate the line because the heavy current will give your streamer plenty of action. Each presentation will take only a few seconds, but you should make several passes through the same pocket before moving along. The idea behind the Brooks Method is that fish living in swift water must make split-second decisions about drifting food sources.

As I mentioned in the introduction, you should not limit your fishing library only to books about your chosen species or technique. The Pocket Water Method for bass is a useful technique gleaned from the writings of other anglers and applied to my own fly-fishing situation.

Bottom Streamers for Moving Water

The weight and overall size of your bottom streamers are more important than the hook size. Carry bottom streamers that are between 2 and 5 inches long. Vary the weight of your bottom streamers by using different sizes of beads and dumbbell eyes. If you are fishing in low-visibility water, consider adding a "hot spot" to some of your bottom streamers by tying in a bright fluorescent wing or body.

Equipment for Bottom Streamers in Creeks and Rivers

Present bottom streamers on creeks and rivers with an 8- or 9-weight, 9-foot fast-action graphite fly rod. Pack a spool of 8- to 14-pound-test fluorocarbon leader material to cut your leaders from. Leaders in slow current should be at least as long as the water depth, and swift water will require leaders about twice as long as the depth of the water. Be sure to keep an assortment of strike indicators in your box of bottom streamers.

Nymphing for Bass

Believe it or not, you can catch bass on nymphs. Smallmouth bass seem more apt to take nymphs, though I have caught a handful of largemouth bass on nymphs as well. Using a large, buoyant strike indicator and a long leader, set up your tackle so that the nymph will drift just off the bottom. Cast over deep bottom structure that holds bass during cold water periods, and simply allow the rig to drift on the current. Feed as much line into the drift as you can without disturbing the nymph, then pick up and cast again. Even in northern climates, nymphing can extend the bass season into a year-round affair.

Nymphs for Bass

Nymphing for bass is not like nymphing for trout. There is no need for exact anatomical replicas of local nymphs, and tiny nymphs are ineffective. Instead, opt for large, nondescript nymphs that cover a range of possible prey. Tie lightly weighted Gold-Ribbed Hare's Ears, Girdle Bugs, and Woolly Buggers in various colors. Mustad 3366 or equivalent hooks in sizes 8 through 2 are an excellent choice.

Equipment Used to Nymph for Bass

Use a standard 8-weight, 9-foot graphite rod to nymph for bass. You will need a weight-forward, floating fly line, a long fluorocarbon leader, and a strike indicator that is buoyant enough to support the leader and the nymph.

Bass Success in Cool Water

Like all fish, bass are cold-blooded animals. Their body temperatures are directly affected by the temperature of the surrounding water. This is why bass become sluggish in cold water and more active as the water warms up. If you understand this, you can alter your presentation as the seasons change and continue to hook up bass well into autumn.

When water temperatures drop below about 60°F, bass begin to slow down their feeding. They hug the bottoms of streams and lakes, soaking up the last of the warm water, and are not likely to rise to top-water bass bugs. If you are not having much luck, check the temperature of the water. You might be surprised to see how cold the water is in early spring when the air feels so warm. Likewise, a warm winter day will

have less effect on the water temperature, so don't let the air temperature fool you. Check the water temperature. If it is below 60°F, I recommend putting your bass-bug box back in your vest. Try a subsurface
technique like streamers or nymphs instead.

Fighting Bass on Fly Tackle

Both largemouth and smallmouth bass are strong fish, prized for their
tough fighting abilities. Smallmouth bass are well known for their aerial displays, but largemouth bass can jump and tail-walk with the best
bronzebacks. Keeping a tight line on bass is an important part of landing these battlers. If you allow slack line to form, you will give the fish
an opportunity to throw your hook. Make your decision early in the
fight whether you will land the bass on the reel or off the reel so that
you can concentrate on keeping a tight line on the fish. Use your rod to
wear down the bass and to steer it away from cover where it can break
off your leader. Bass fight tenaciously but tire quickly, so be ready for a
street brawl, not a twelve-round fight.

Catch-and-Release and the Future of Bass Angling

The popularity of catch-and-release has grown to the extent that some
anglers release every fish. Catch-and-release is the preferred method
among 100 percent of all bass polled, but it also ensures that there
will be quality sportfishing in the future. Don't believe it? Here is a
personal example that should be the rule, rather than the exception,
across the country.

When I lived in Indiana, one of the local streams enacted a minimum 20-inch limit for all smallmouth bass. This essentially created
a catch-and-release-only smallmouth fishery that quickly became
one of the premiere angling destinations in the state. That stream is
the gorgeous Sugar Creek in Montgomery County. Fifteen years ago
Sugar Creek was not even on the map as far as quality fishing is concerned. Today, thanks to the efforts of the Indiana DNR to promote
catch-and-release, Sugar Creek is one of the finest smallmouth bass
streams in the entire Midwest. You might think that killing one bass

does not hurt the population, but where would we be if everybody felt the same?

Protecting this valuable resource begins at the fly-tying vise. You will greatly reduce the damage inflicted on caught fish by de-barbing your hooks as you tie bass flies. Bass fought properly on a tight line stand little chance of throwing the hook, regardless of whether there is a barb or not. Large barbs on your fly hooks can actually keep you from setting the hook effectively. If the hook only penetrates to the barb, you have a bass hooked on less than a quarter-inch of iron! Rather than rely on a barb to hold your fish, de-barb your hooks and sharpen them with a hook hone. Even if you have hooked a bass deeply, removing a barbless hook is a snap with hemostats or a hook-removal tool.

Bass are more resilient than trout and typically do not need to be revived before release. The best way to handle a bass is to grip the fish by its lower jaw, which immobilizes the bass. If possible, simply slide the hook from the fish's mouth and release it without removing it from the water. If you must remove the fish from the water, lift it straight up by the lower jaw. Do not hold a bass horizontally by the lower jaw without supporting the fish's body because you could damage or break the fish's jaw. Never pick up a bass by sticking your fingers into its gills. This is a death sentence for any fish.

Sometimes you will land a bass that is mortally wounded or beat to the point that it cannot be revived. This is rare with bass, but it does happen on occasion. If you catch a bass that is really whipped, bleeding from the gills, or gut-hooked, then kill it and enjoy a good meal. Catch-and-release is important, but wanton waste of fish is not the goal.

Bass are the most popular freshwater gamefish in the country, but there is no guarantee that we will always enjoy great bass fishing. If you fish on waters where closed seasons or size limits are in effect, it is your responsibility as a sportsman or sportswoman to observe these regulations. The culture of catch-and-eat has changed dramatically over the years, and it is exciting to see so many fantastic bass fisheries grow where there were once only decimated populations of small fish.

BASS FLIES

Dahlberg Diver

Hook: Mustad C52S BLN or equivalent stinger
Thread: Ultra Thread 210 Denier
Tail: Bucktail, squirrel tail, or hackle feathers
Body: Spun-and-clipped deer belly hair
Eyes: Plastic doll eyes, attached with Goop
Note: There are limitless variations of the Dahlberg Diver, but they all feature a tapered nose and high collar that cause the fly to dive when retrieved.

Deer Hair Slider

Hook: Mustad C52S BLN or equivalent stinger
Thread: Ultra Thread 210 Denier
Tail: Six splayed hackle feathers
Body: Spun-and-clipped deer belly hair
Eyes: Plastic doll eyes, attached with Goop
Note: Unlike Dahlberg Divers, the slider has a long taper and sparse collar that allows the fly to dive quietly when a subtle presentation is required.

Tap's Bug

Hook: Mustad C52S BLN or equivalent stinger
Thread: Ultra Thread 210 Denier
Tail: Bucktail
Body: Spun-and-clipped deer belly hair
Note: Add a layer or two of Sally Hansen's Hard As Nails fingernail polish to the face of this one to make it really pop.

Holschlag Hackle Fly

Hook: Mustad R75-79580 or equivalent streamer
Thread: Danville's Flymaster 70 Denier
Eyes: Dumbbell eyes painted red
Tail: Marabou
Flash: Krystal Flash
Legs: Round rubber
Hackle: Hen hackle
Body: Dyed rabbit dubbing
Note: Though not exactly the original pattern, this version of Tim's Holschlag Hackle Fly catches a lot bass.

Mixed Media Crayfish

Hook: Mustad R75-79580 or equivalent streamer
Thread: Danville's Flymaster 70 Denier
Eyes: Lead dumbbell eyes
Tail: Rubber spinner-bait skirt material
Body: Dyed rabbit dubbing
Wing: Fox squirrel
Note: Tie the rubber skirt material in at the nose and secure it along the length of the hook shank, like you are tying a Clouser Minnow. The original version of this fly features a thread body and fox-fur wing, but I think this one is more durable and it still works great.

Half-and-Half

Hook: Mustad S71SZ-34007 or equivalent big-game
Thread: Ultra Thread 210 Denier
Eyes: Lead dumbbell eyes
Tail: Six hackle feathers
Belly: White bucktail
Flash: Krystal Flash
Wing: Dark bucktail
Head: 5-minute epoxy
Note: This classic combination of the Clouser Minnow and Lefty's Deceiver catches bass from coast to coast. Tie it with various amounts of weight to fish deeper or shallower depending on conditions.

Foam Head Streamer

Hook: Mustad C52S BLN or equivalent stinger
Thread: Ultra Thread 210 Denier
Weight: Several turns of non-lead wire at the front of hook
Tail: Rabbit zonker strip
Foul guard: Loop of heavy monofilament tied over tail, then pull tail through
Body: Marabou
Head: Craft foam, cut to shape and hot-glued to hook
Eyes: Plastic doll eyes, attached with Goop
Note: This is a great fly for beginners to start out with because it allows them to form a large head without having to worry about spinning deer hair. By varying the amount of weight you tie under the head, you can make this streamer swim near the surface or down deep.

Bead-Head Woolly Bugger

Hook: Mustad R75-79580 or equivalent streamer
Thread: Danville's Flymaster 70 Denier
Bead: Brass, sized to fit your hook
Weight: Several turns of non-lead wire pushed into the bead
Tail: Marabou
Hackle: Hen hackle or large, webby rooster
Body: Dyed rabbit dubbing
Note: The Woolly Bugger is probably the most versatile fly around. Keep them around in several colors and weights and you'll catch plenty of fish.

Skittish Crayfish

Hook: Mustad R75-79580 or equivalent streamer
Thread: Danville's Flymaster 70 Denier
Eyes: Lead dumbbell eyes
Claws: Dyed bucktail
Flash: Krystal Flash
Head: Dyed rabbit dubbing
Carapace: Moose body hair, folded over to form carapace and tail
Rib: Copper wire
Body and legs: Rabbit zonker strip, palmered
Note: I've been tweaking this one for years. Tie the eyes near the hook bend, and work this fly slowly along the bottom.

Rubber Leg Crease Fly

Hook: Mustad R75-79580 or equivalent streamer
Thread: Danville's Flymaster 70 Denier
Flash: Krystal Flash
Tail: Hackle feathers
Body: Craft foam, cut to shape and hot-glued to hook
Legs: Round rubber
Eyes: Plastic doll eyes, attached with Goop
Note: Another simple fly that catches a lot of bass and is great for beginners. The rubber legs wiggle enticingly even when the fly is at rest.

Gurgler

Hook: Mustad R75-79580 or equivalent streamer
Thread: Danville's Flymaster 70 Denier
Tail: Bucktail
Flash: Krystal Flash
Back: Craft foam, cut in a strip, tied in backward, then folded over
Legs: Round rubber
Body: Polar Ice Dubbing
Gurgling head: Excess foam from the back, tied in and clipped off
Note: This is another easy one that allows beginners to produce a noisy fly without the hassle of spinning deer hair.

Crease Fly

Hook: Mustad R75-79580 or equivalent streamer

Tail: Bucktail and Flashabou

Body: Craft foam, cut to shape and hot-glued to body

Eyes: Doll eyes, attached with Goop

Note: You can get creative with this one. Color the body with Sharpie markers to imitate your favorite spinning lures, or coat the fly with 5-minute epoxy for a shiny finish.

CHAPTER 6

Panfish

It would be pretty easy to dismiss fishing for panfish as a childish pastime. After all, panfish are easy to catch, they are small in comparison to other gamefish, and practically every one of us began our angling careers doing battle with 4-inch bluegills on a Snoopy pole. It's a piece of cake, right?

Sure, it's easy to pick off plenty of little bluegills at the local park, but have you ever targeted *big* bluegills? If you have, then you know that an honest 1-pounder can be as rare as a 20-inch rainbow trout. The same goes for serious crappie anglers. Filling a stringer with crappies is like shooting layups when they are spawning, but catching papermouths in midsummer isn't so easy.

Fly fishing for panfish is what you make of it. Whether you are catching a bucketful of little guys from the end of a dock or hunting trophy 'gills from a bass boat, fly fishing for panfish is an enjoyable way to spend time on the water and catch some fish. In this chapter we'll have a look at the equipment and techniques that you can use to catch plenty of panfish. We'll also dig a little deeper into the business of targeting trophy-size panfish when they are spawning as well as when they are not

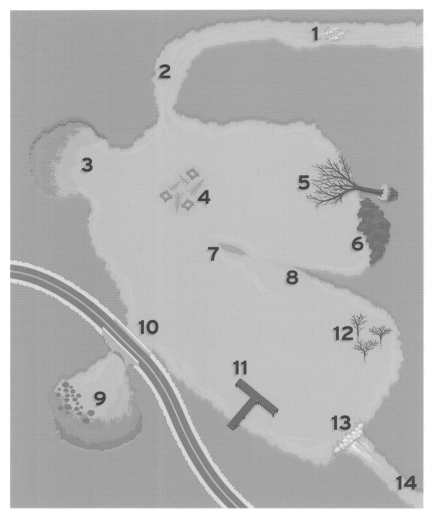

Where to fly fish for panfish:

1. Riffles

2. Deep pool in stream bend

3. Shallow bay with submerged vegetation, reeds, and cattails

4. Man-made structure like fish cribs and sunken Christmas trees (these are often noted on DNR websites and maps of reservoirs along with relative depths)

5. Fallen timber

6. Overhanging brush

7. Hump or saddle

8. Point

9. Swampy backwater

10. Around bridge pilings

11. Docks and piers (crappie hot spot)

12. Standing timber (crappie hot spot)

13. Riprap dam face

14. Tailwater below dam

CRAPPIES

Crappies are a temperamental species. One day you can't unhook them fast enough to keep up with the bite, and the next day you get skunked. The pre-spawn run is a great chance to catch a lot of crappies, but many anglers simply pick this low-hanging fruit and forget about crappies once summer hits. If you understand why crappies move and where they go, you will not only catch more fish, but you can catch crappies after everyone else has given up on them.

The key to crappie fly-fishing success does not lie in special equipment or top-secret flies. You just need to understand what drives crappies as they migrate, suspend, and school in a given body of water. Let's take a look at how crappies behave in different conditions and how you can get them to take a fly.

Pre-Spawn Crappies in Lakes

Springtime crappies begin moving from the deeper water into shallow bays and shorelines as the water temperature rises into the upper 40s or lower 50s. The initial movements are driven by food rather than

This is a black (as opposed to white) crappie.

spawning. Shallow areas that are protected from the wind and receive lots of sunshine warm up before other parts of the lake. This causes a population explosion among the microscopic organisms that minnows and baitfish feed on. Of course, when the baitfish arrive to feed, crappies are not far behind.

You can take advantage of these pre-spawn feeding runs by identifying shallow, protected bays that routinely receive a lot of sun in the spring. Focus your early-season crappie-fishing efforts on these areas. If you find a good spot for pre-spawn crappies, mark it on your map because there is a good chance that they will return to the same place over and over again.

Pre-Spawn Staging and Spawning in Lakes

Crappies move out of deeper water and begin staging in shallow spawning waters when the water temperature is consistently in the 50s. The fish will continue to venture into the shallowest water to feed, but are just as likely to suspend over structure where the shallow water drops off to deeper water. If you catch a few crappies in the shallows at this time, be sure to fish the drop-off thoroughly to pick up suspended fish.

Most of the excitement surrounding the crappie spawning run is really centered around the pre-spawn staging period. The actual spawn takes place over a day or two, and crappies are much less likely to feed during spawning. I'll leave it to you to decide whether or not you want to fish to spawning crappies. I don't do it because I think that bothering spawning crappies puts undue pressure on fish that are already stressed, even when you release them. Unless you fish a lake every day or have strange luck, you probably won't encounter crappies that are actually "in the act" of spawning. If you do, consider limiting your keep that day because overharvest during the spawn can affect crappie size and population down the road.

Post-Spawn Crappies in Lakes

Once their reproductive duties are fulfilled, crappies drop back into deeper water and become very oriented to structure and cover. They will continue to make feeding runs into shallow water, so keep hitting the shelves and drop-offs near early-season feeding grounds. Summer crappies will move into thick vegetation such as reeds, cabbage, and cattails in search of baitfish. Like the springtime feeding runs, summer crappies make raids into the vegetation then retreat to deeper water. Unlike the early-season runs, summer crappies make their raids into cover and shallow water when the sun is low in the sky then move deeper as full sunlight is on the water. Fish the shallows for summer crappies in the early morning or late evening. As the sun rises in the sky, fish deeper structure and cover that is adjacent to the area where you caught crappies earlier.

Summer Crappies in Lakes

Summer crappie fishing can be the best of times or the worst of times. Crappies leave their easy-to-find spawning shallows and move into deeper water. They suspend at various depths depending on water temperatures, sunlight penetration, and the availability of food. Fortunately for fly anglers, crappies are not true open-water fish. They do not cruise deep, featureless water like striped bass. Instead, crappies suspend over structure near the same type of water that attracts them during the pre-spawn feeding runs and the actual spawning period. While crappies do move into deeper water when water temperatures rise, they do not actually move into true "open water." Al Linder called crappies "confined water" fish because they move into deeper water but continue to relate to structure and cover.

Do you remember when you marked those honey holes where you caught the first springtime crappies? Start there, fishing the deeper water over drop-offs and structure like rock piles, ledges, and submerged points. In general, the crappies will move deeper along the structure as water temperatures rise and when the sun is brighter. Focus your summertime crappie fly-fishing efforts on these areas of descending structure in the early morning and late evening for the best catch.

Crappies in Rivers

Crappie fishing in lakes is very popular and productive, but you can also catch a mess of crappies in rivers. It is important to note that crappies do not flourish in swiftly moving water. You can catch a few crappies in classic riffle-run-pool water, but sloughs and backwaters are the real sweet spots for crappie in river environments. These areas generally have little current, which favors the production of big crappies. Backwaters are frequently studded with trees, vegetation, and woody cover that make for excellent crappie habitat.

Although part of a river system, you can treat these slack-water areas like small lakes. Big, mature rivers like the Ohio, the Upper Mississippi, and the lower Wabash feature flooded backwaters, cuts, and sloughs that function as reservoirs for the massive amounts of water that move through these systems. Target these areas for maximum crappie success and be sure to follow the same principles of structure and cover, water temperature, spawning habitat, light penetration, and food availability.

Equipment for Crappie Fly Fishing

Crappies are willing biters, but not renown for their fighting abilities. A lighter fly-fishing outfit will make better sport of crappie angling, but be careful not to go so light that you cannot cast and present medium-size streamers to the fish.

Fly Rods

A moderate to moderate-fast action 4-weight rod between 7½ and 9 feet long will allow you to cast streamers and still provide plenty of sport.

Lines and Leaders

A weight-forward floating fly line is the best all-around choice for crappie fishing. You might find a sinking-tip or a full-sink line useful in the summer, but it is really not necessary.

Use knotless tapered monofilament leaders for surface and near-surface presentations. If you are fishing to crappies in deeper water, switch to a level fluorocarbon leader at least twice as long as the depth of the water. A strike indicator at the line-to-leader connection will help you pick up light crappie strikes when you are fishing deep.

Flies

Crappies are fish eaters, so your crappie fly box should have plenty of streamers. Pack along lots of Clouser Minnows and jig flies in a variety of weights. Clouser Minnows with bead-chain eyes are great for spring crappies in shallow water. As the fish move toward deeper structure, switch to heavier lead-eye Clousers and jig flies. Marabou crappie jigs used for spin fishing are too heavy to comfortably cast with a 4-weight fly rod, but you can easily tie similar jig flies using 1/64- and 1/100-ounce trout jigs. Color combinations of chartreuse and white, red and yellow, and black and yellow are always top producers.

Presenting Flies to Crappies

Think middle-level water when you are fishing for crappies with a fly rod. Crappies tend to look up when they are feeding, though they are not as apt to take top-water flies as other panfish. You should present your crappie flies at or slightly above the fish's level. You can do this with or without a strike indicator.

Strike-Indicator Crappie Fishing

There are a couple of ways to fly fish for crappies with a strike indicator. One method is to simply attach a twist-on or peg-on indicator at the line-to-leader connection and fish streamers with a standard retrieve. You can also present jig flies by suspending them under an indicator. Tie a yarn indicator to your leader, then add a separate length of tippet and attach your fly to it. Be sure that your jig fly is not so heavy that it sinks the indicator. When you cast this rig, the jig fly will suspend horizontally right below the indicator. You can twitch the indicator to give your fly action or simply let it sit. This is the fly angler's version of a spinning angler's "float and fly" rig, and it is deadly for crappies.

Set up your indicator so that the fly will suspend at or slightly above the level which the crappies are holding. If you can't see the fish, set up your rig so that the fly is shallower rather than deeper. Cast as close to cover as you can without hanging up, and let your fly sink. Retrieve your crappie rig slowly, allowing the fly to settle after each strip. When crappies are aggressively biting, they often take the fly before it can sink all the way.

Catching Crappies with Swimming Streamers

Crappies are fish-eaters, so actively retrieved swimming streamers are a natural choice when you are going after papermouths. Lightly weighted swimming streamers are the best option in most situations. You may need to throw a heavy streamer when fish are suspended deep, but crappies become increasingly difficult targets for fly anglers as they move deeper.

The old "if you only had one fly . . ." debate has pretty much been beaten to death, but I will confidently tell you that if a chartreuse-and-white Clouser Minnow doesn't work, you're going to need bait and a bobber to catch crappies that day. Carry Clousers in a range of weights so that some sink slowly and others go straight to the bottom. Cast in tight to woody cover and strip the fly out quickly. Then hit the same spot and retrieve slower so that reluctant crappies can have another look. If you are fishing to crappies suspended over structure, use the two-cast method so that you can fish the front of the cover without putting your fly line over any fish that are hanging there. Crappies form loose schools around cover and structure, so keep fishing a hot spot as long as you're catching fish. When a crappie bite is on, you can literally catch a fish on every cast.

Catching and Keeping Crappies

Many crappies have escaped the frying pan when anglers try to lift them out of the water by the leader and the fish's weight ripped the hook from its mouth. Crappies' mouths are simply too fragile for such treatment. Reel in a caught crappie until you can get a handle on it, then pick up the fish by its lower jaw or by gripping it around the middle of its body. De-barbed hooks are easier to remove when a crappie swallows your fly. Use de-barbed hooks even if you plan on keeping your catch because you won't want to waste time dealing with a gut-hooked fish in the middle of a heavy bite. A net might seem like a good idea, but it will also slow you down when the crappies are really biting.

If you are keeping a mess of crappies, you will need a stringer or a fish basket. When you have to hike in or move around a lot, a simple stringer is best. If you are fishing from a boat or a dock, you can use a wire fish basket. Fish baskets are easier to use and keep the fish alive longer.

BLUEGILL

Bluegills are almost everywhere. It doesn't take a lot of effort to catch plenty of small bluegills, but hooking up trophy-size fish on a fly rod can

Bluegills are small, colorful fish that are fun to catch on light fly-fishing tackle.

be just as challenging as landing a big trout. Bluegills have tiny mouths and usually cannot eat large food sources such as minnows or crayfish. They favor insects, larvae, snails, and other tiny aquatic invertebrates. This inclination makes bluegills a natural target for anglers wielding lightweight fly-fishing outfits.

Like crappies, bluegills and other panfish begin moving into shallow water in the spring when water temperatures start to rise. Pre-spawn bluegills go where the food is, which is often sun-drenched shallows and the warm, windswept edges of lakes and ponds. Look for the warmest water and you will find pre-spawn bluegills.

It is easy to pick out their round, stony nests as you walk around the banks of a pond. Small bluegills often stick around their nests for several weeks. However, the biggest bluegills didn't get big by hanging around shallow water. They move into the spawning grounds, take care

Wrap your palm around the top of a bluegill when you land it to avoid getting pricked by the spiny dorsal fin.

of business, and head for cover or deep water. If it is big bluegills that you're after, you probably won't catch too many by fishing the nests.

Post-spawn bluegills move off of the nests and suspend on drop-offs just like crappies. They may raid the shallows in the early morning or evening, but the best bluegills will be suspended in deeper water off of submerged points, drop-offs, and around deep structure. Bluegills are also attracted to cover. Overhanging brush, fallen timber, sunken logs, standing stumps, and submerged trees are all prime examples of woody cover that attracts bluegills. Man-made cover like docks, pilings, piers, and bridges are also bluegill magnets.

In creeks and rivers most bluegills seek slack water. However, there are always some hardy bluegills that spend their days in the current. You will find these tough bluegills hanging around woody cover, in current eddies, and in the deeper water on the outside of river bends. Life in the current makes these bluegills fight like fish twice their size.

Equipment for Bluegill Fly Fishing

While bluegills are tough fighters, they don't get very big compared to other warmwater gamefish. A 9-foot, 2-weight rod will provide great sport for bluegill fishing. Fly-rod outfits over 4-weight are a little too heavy to make bluegill fishing interesting. A knotless tapered monofilament leader is perfect for all but the deepest bluegill presentations.

Dry flies, panfish poppers, foam spiders, nymphs, wet flies, and tiny streamers are all effective bluegill flies. Bluegills are not selective and will usually try to eat anything that will fit in their mouths. Bluegills are very likely to swallow flies, so you should de-barb all of your bluegill flies. A pair of hemostats will help you pull flies from deeply hooked bluegills. A strike indicator is a must for subsurface bluegills.

Presenting Flies to Bluegills

Bluegills are a very forgiving species. If you blow a cast and it splashes down 5 feet from your target, go ahead and fish it out. There is a good chance that some curious bluegill will cruise over and take your fly anyway. There are several effective ways to present flies to

Bluegills have tiny mouths and take small flies.

bluegills depending on the conditions, the fish, and the type of water you are fishing.

The Active Retrieve

You already know that catching bluegills requires small flies. An easy way to catch lots of bluegills on a lake or pond is to use an active retrieve with a panfish popper, wet fly, miniature streamer, or even a dry fly. Bluegills will take many of the same flies that catch trout, though bluegills are not nearly as selective.

Use a small fly to search around weeds and woody cover around the fringes of a lake or pond. You have a better chance of hooking up bigger bluegills if there is deep water near the cover that you are fishing. Use the two-cast technique to fish the near side of the cover first, and then fish your fly through the cover with a second cast. Vary the action of your fly from nearly dead-still to a steady chug to determine the mood of the bluegills.

You can actively retrieve any type of fly when fishing for bluegills, but keep your flies in the size 6 through 14 range so that the fish can easily take your fly. Use buoyant dry flies such as Humpies and Irresistibles when you are employing an active retrieve because they will stay afloat much longer than standard dry flies. Don't be afraid to use a small strike indicator to help you detect subsurface bites if you are using wet flies or miniature streamers.

The Dead Drift

You can have a lot of fun and practice your trout-angling skills by dead-drifting wet or dry flies for bluegills in warmwater streams. If you are not familiar with the term, a dead drift is a fly presentation in which the fly line is manipulated so that the fly appears to be floating along free of the line. Whether you are fishing wet flies or dry flies, the keys to a good dead-drift presentation are reading the currents, anticipating the drift of your fly, and controlling the fly line so that drag does not cause your fly to move unnaturally.

Mastering the art of the dead drift can take many seasons for trout anglers, but bluegills are infinitely less demanding. Bluegills are just as likely to take a size 8 spider fly skating across the current as they are a perfectly matched, flawlessly presented dry fly. As long as you put your fly near some bluegills, you stand a good chance of getting a strike.

Use the dead-drift technique to search for bluegills near cover and structure on warmwater streams. Woody cover like fallen trees, standing stumps, and overhanging branches are great places to drift a bluegill fly. Backwaters, eddies, and current seams will hold some of the biggest bluegills, too. Make the best dead-drift presentation that you can to these places, and you are sure to hook up some nice bluegills.

Don't overlook the usefulness of the dead-drift presentation on still waters either. Anyone who has ever tossed a bobber-and-bait for bluegills knows that the best bite often comes quickly when the bait hits the water. Use the same technique with a fly rod to pick up bluegills in prime still-water areas like lily pads, woody cover, and rocky points. Just cast your fly near the cover or structure and wait. You will see the take on a surface fly or you can use a strike indicator to control depth and detect takes for subsurface flies. Give each cast a minute or two, then retrieve the fly and let it settle again. This allows you to present the fly to fish in several positions around the lie on a single cast.

Strike Indicators and Bluegills

Strike indicators are an important part of bluegill fly-fishing techniques. Perhaps more than any other species, you can dramatically increase your catch by using a strike indicator in conjunction with these methods. Bluegills are small fish, have small mouths, and frequently nibble at a fly or bait before taking it. Like many other warmwater gamefish, they are likely to be found suspended at a specific depth depending on conditions such as water temperature and light penetration. A strike indicator simplifies both of these situations by allowing you to see subsurface strikes when they happen, as well as giving you the ability to

Even the most devoted trout angler would have to admit that pumpkinseed bluegills are beautiful fish.

suspend your fly at a specific depth. I strongly suggest that you buy a few strike indicators and keep them with your bluegill flies.

Fly Fishing for Bluegills with Kids

Even if you are a dyed-in-the-wool big-game angler, you have to admit that bluegills and kids go together like apple pie and the Fourth of July. There is no better way to introduce kids to fly fishing, outdoor sports, and the natural world in general than by taking them fly fishing for bluegills. Although we have discussed many ways that you can target the biggest bluegills, kids are thrilled to catch *any* fish, and bluegills are ready and willing to take a fly. Lifting 4-inch bluegills from a 2-foot-wide creek might not qualify as high sport for an experienced angler, but it lays the foundation for a lifetime of outdoor fun for kids who are lucky enough to have someone take them fishing.

Catching bluegills is the perfect way to introduce kids to fly fishing.

107

PANFISH FLIES

Mini Muddler Minnow

Hook: Tiemco 200R or equivalent curved-shank hook
Thread: Danville's Flymaster 70 Denier
Tail: Bucktail
Body: Gold tinsel
Wing: Bucktail
Head: Spun-and-clipped deer hair

Black Gnat

Hook: Mustad R50-94840 or equivalent dry fly
Thread: Danville's Flymaster 70 Denier, black
Wings: Matching sections of gray duck primary feathers
Tail: Black hackle fibers
Body: Dry-fly dubbing
Hackle: Black genetic hackle

Bead-Head Prince Nymph

Hook: Mustad 9671 or equivalent wet fly
Thread: Danville's Flymaster 70 Denier
Head: Tungsten copper bead
Tail: Brown goose biots
Rib: Gold wire
Body: Peacock herl
Wings: White goose biots
Hackle: Brown hen hackle

Bead-Head Squirrel Nymph

Hook: Mustad 9671 or equivalent wet fly
Head: Brass or tungsten bead
Thread: Danville's Flymaster 70 Denier
Tail: Mallard flank fibers
Rib: Copper wire
Body: Squirrel dubbing
Thorax: Polar ice dubbing

Royal Coachman

Hook: Mustad 9671 or equivalent wet fly
Thread: Danville's Flymaster 70 Denier
Tail: Golden pheasant tippets
Body: Peacock herl and red floss
Hackle: Brown hen hackle
Wing: White calf tail

Partridge and Orange

Hook: Mustad 9671 or equivalent wet fly
Thread: Danville's Flymaster 70 Denier
Body: Orange floss
Hackle: Partridge

Bluegill Spider

Hook: Tiemco 200R or equivalent
curved-shank hook
Thread: Danville's Flymaster 70 Denier
Body: Craft foam, cut to shape
Legs: Round rubber

Panfish Popper

Hook: Tiemco 200R or equivalent curved-shank hook
Thread: Danville's Flymaster 70 Denier
Head: Styrofoam, painted and coated with 5-minute epoxy
Tail: Craft Fur
Flash: Flashabou
Hackle: Webby rooster hackle

Panfish Slider

Hook: Tiemco 200R or equivalent curved-shank hook
Thread: Danville's Flymaster 70 Denier
Head: Styrofoam, painted and coated with 5-minute epoxy
Tail: Craft Fur
Flash: Flashabou
Hackle: Webby rooster hackle

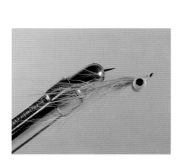

Note: There are probably a million ways to make panfish poppers and sliders. I like to carve the heads out of regular packing Styrofoam with a double-edged razor, hot-glue them to the hook shank, and then paint, add eyes, and coat with epoxy. It takes a while to do it this way, but you can make them exactly how you want them.

Clouser Minnow

Hook: Mustad S71SZ-34007 or equivalent; use size 4 or smaller for crappies
Thread: Danville's Flymaster 70 Denier
Eyes: Lead dumbbell
Belly: White bucktail
Wing: Chartreuse bucktail
Head: 5-minute epoxy

Bead-Chain Clouser Minnow

Hook: Mustad S71SZ-34007 or equivalent; use size 4 or smaller for crappies
Thread: Danville's Flymaster 70 Denier
Eyes: Bead chain
Belly: White bucktail
Wing: Chartreuse bucktail
Head: 5-minute epoxy

Note: Clouser Minnows catch all kinds of fish all over the world. Tie them smaller for crappies or larger for bass and stripers. Varying the amount of bucktail and the type of eyes will allow you to fish Clousers shallow or deep.

CHAPTER 7

Pike and Muskellunge

Let's say that you caught a 24-inch smallmouth on a fly. You would probably get your picture in the newspaper and be the envy of all your fly-fishing pals. Now let's say that it was a 24-inch pike or muskellunge. Most folks would tell you to toss it back so that it could grow up. That's how big pike and muskies get, and they are not exclusive to the Canadian wilderness. You can catch pike and muskellunge across much of the northern United States, but it takes some special equipment and a lot of dedication to go after these apex predators on a regular basis. Get your wire leaders and jaw spreaders ready, because we are about to go where the big fish live.

PIKE AND MUSKELLUNGE: WHAT'S THE DIFFERENCE?

It can sometimes be difficult to distinguish between pike and muskellunge. Generally speaking, pike are olive green with light spots. Muskellunge are usually silvery green with dark spots. Muskies occur in distinct phases and their markings can vary from clear silver to heavily barred bright green.

Muskellunge can grow much bigger than the average pike in the same water, but they do not fare well in waters that have large pike populations. Environmental aspects such as the lack of large prey or

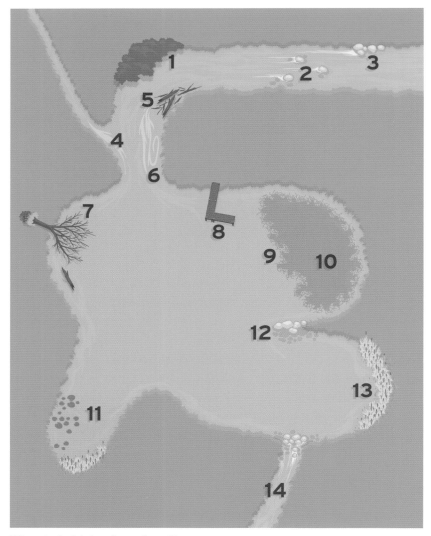

Where to fly fish for pike and muskie:

1. Overhanging brush on river or creek
2. Boulders (pocket water)
3. Rocky outcroppings
4. Coldwater feeder streams (summertime northern pike hot spot)
5. Logjams
6. Current eddy
7. Fallen timber and sunken logs
8. Docks and piers
9. Edges around submerged weed beds
10. Over fresh, green weed beds
11. Shallow bays near deep water
12. Rocky points
13. Reeds and cattails
14. Cool-water tailrace below dam

substantial cover may limit the number of muskies in lakes and rivers, while pike populations are less affected by these factors. Pike also hatch and mature earlier than muskies, so a lot of muskie fry are eaten by larger pike fry. As a result, pike are abundant in many lakes and rivers, while muskellunge are a far more rare catch.

Fortunately for anglers, there are enough similarities between the two major members of the Esox clan that it is not necessary to make a major distinction between pike and muskie fishing. Both species are large, toothy ambush-predators that feast on fish ranging from small minnows to nice-size bass. Both are extremely aggressive feeders, although muskies seem a bit less inclined to consistently take flies than their reckless cousins. As far as we're concerned, however, the most important trait shared by pike and muskie is the tendency of both species to rely on heavy cover for attacking their prey. Locating prime ambush cover and fishing it with aggressive determination are the keys to successful pike and muskellunge fly fishing.

PIKE AND MUSKELLUNGE THROUGH THE SEASONS

Northern pike move from deep wintering structure into shallow areas to feed and spawn as springtime water temperatures hit 45°F. Muskellunge follow shortly after, spawning when water temperatures are around 50°F. This is an important factor in determining the quality of muskie fishing in a particular body of water. Few muskie fry survive the frenzied feeding of larger northern pike fry.

Unlike many warmwater gamefish that guard their nests, pike and muskellunge spawn and move on. They still frequent shallow water in the spring, but may not be near the area where spawning occurred. Instead, they come to the warm shallows to take up ambush points among woody cover and weed beds. Shallow aquatic vegetation begins to grow earlier than weeds in deeper water, and both species take advantage of the baitfish and smaller gamefish that are attracted to the emergent cover. Concentrate your springtime pike and muskie fishing on submerged and emergent weeds when water temperatures are around 60°F to 70°F.

Muskellunge continue to feed around woody cover, rocky structure, and aquatic vegetation as water temperatures near 80°F. However, summer water temperatures send big pike looking for cooler water. Springs, deep runs, and coldwater feeder creeks attract the biggest northern pike when the water starts to warm up. Focus your attention on these areas if you are after trophy pike in the summer.

Pike and muskellunge can be especially difficult to locate during the dog days of summer. Look for them around deep structure like submerged creek beds and drop-offs in lakes, or deep outside bends and rocky runs in rivers and creeks. Like most warmwater gamefish, pike and muskie eventually look for cooler, more oxygenated water when temperatures rise.

Autumn can be a glorious time to fish for pike and muskie. As water temperatures begin to cool down, the fish again move into weedy shallows to feed. Be sure to fish all of the likely structure and cover, but pay special attention to patches of aquatic vegetation that stay green. These bits of healthy cover support the best populations of baitfish, with pike and muskie sure to be nearby.

Pike and muskellunge suspend along drop-offs and over deep weed beds as winter approaches. Lake fishing for pike and muskies is mostly finished at this point for fly-rodders, but a warm stretch can bring a few fish within casting range into early winter. If there is an open winter season where you live, you will find the best fishing for pike and muskies in weedy shallows on warm winter days.

PIKE AND MUSKELLUNGE HABITATS

Pike and muskies are extremely oriented to structure and cover. Locating the best areas of a particular body of water is the first step to pike and muskie success. Let's have a look at the best places to find them.

Weedy Cover

Weed beds are a prime ambush location for pike and muskie. Cabbage weed is the best weedy cover for muskies. Patches of this common aquatic

Pike and muskies have big mouths full of teeth. CHAD RAICH

vegetation should be fished thoroughly from several angles. Other types of aquatic vegetation will hold both pike and muskies as well. Pay special attention to open channels and pockets in weed beds because pike and muskie will tuck into these little nooks to ambush passing baitfish. You should look for full, healthy green weed beds because they will hold the best baitfish and gamefish populations. Patches of sparse, brown vegetation are not very likely to harbor big pike and muskellunge.

Emergent vegetation such as reeds and cattails will hold pike and muskies as well. This type of weedy cover is common around the edges of lakes and in slack-water areas of large rivers. Reeds and cattails are a dead giveaway that shallow water is nearby, and shallow water can hold large numbers of early- and late-season baitfish and gamefish. Look for pike and muskies in the shallow waters around these widespread types of cover.

Woody Cover

Like other warmwater gamefish, pike and muskellunge are frequently found around woody cover. They are attracted to woody cover by abundant baitfish and overhead protection. Thick woody cover, such as the submerged branches of a fallen tree, is a great place to pick up pike and

Pike and muskie will try every trick in the book to toss your fly, as this acrobatic northern demonstrates. CHAD RAICH

muskies. Likewise, you will find pike and muskies around sunken logs and dead, submerged standing timber.

Weedy Bays near Deep Water

Weedy bays that gradually drop off into deep water are another top producer of pike and muskellunge. The transition from shallow to deep water provides a varying concentration of aquatic vegetation. In a shallow bay the vegetation is thick and often emergent, which attracts baitfish and gamefish. The vegetation becomes gradually less dense as you move into deeper water because deep water is cooler and sunlight does not penetrate the depths. These factors combine to provide an ideal location for predator fish. Baitfish move into the area that best suits their needs depending on the water temperature, time of day, or the season. Gamefish, including pike and muskellunge, also move in because of the ideal conditions and the abundance of prey. These movements can occur daily, such as when fish move into deeper water as the sun rises higher, or they may be seasonal, such as feeding runs into warmer shallow water in the spring.

Transition Areas

Gradual, weedy fringes are great spots for pike and muskies, but there are other transition areas that will hold fish as well. Sudden

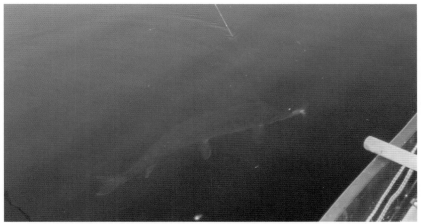

Pike and muskie love to follow flies, so don't be surprised if you hook them right alongside the boat. CHAD RAICH

drop-offs from shallow water to very deep water create a hard edge where weed growth abruptly stops. This hard-edge transition provides a multitude of ideal ambush points for pike and muskies to grab passing baitfish. Swimming beaches at public lakes are often cleared of vegetation to create a better area for swimmers. The perimeter of a swimming area is another example of a hard-edge transition that can hold pike and muskies.

Transition areas are not limited to the edges of a lake or river. Islands are a great example of areas where varying water depths create transition areas away from the main shore. Look for the weedy edge on a mid-lake island for great pike and muskie action. Logjams often form along mid-river islands, creating ideal habitat for pike and muskies as well.

Rocky Cover and Structure

Pike and muskellunge seem to favor weedy cover, but they will take advantage of rocky cover and structure when it is present. This is especially true in large rivers where the current prevents heavy weed growth. Look for rocky areas that stand out from the rest of the terrain. Rocky points, midstream boulders, and submerged rocky shelves are good examples of the type of rocky cover that will hold pike and muskies.

Cradle pike and muskies when you pick them up to support their weight. Be sure to keep your fingers away from those teeth, though! CHAD RAICH

Generally speaking, look for anything that is out of the ordinary when you are fishing rocky cover and structure for pike and muskies. Anomalies in the structure provide ambush points for these large predators, so key in on these spots.

Slack Water

Like other river-dwelling gamefish, pike and muskellunge do not live out their lives in the strongest current. Areas of slack water like backwaters, eddies, and pocket water will hold pike and muskies. You don't necessarily need to locate enormous pockets of slack water to find big pike and muskies. Look for slots and pockets that are just large enough to hold a fish.

Cool Water for Hot-Weather Pike

Unlike muskies, large pike will seek out pockets of cool water when summer weather drives average water temperatures above 55°F or 60°F. Look for sources of cool water if warm water is only producing small pike. Natural springs, deep pockets, and coldwater feeder streams are good sources of cool water. Large pike will congregate around these areas.

FLY-FISHING EQUIPMENT FOR PIKE AND MUSKELLUNGE

Pike and muskellunge are likely the largest freshwater fish that you will ever tackle with a fly rod. Targeting and catching trophy-size pike and muskies requires special equipment. These big, toothy fish will test every component of your fly tackle, not to mention your own strength and angling skills. A standard-fare bass outfit just won't cut the mustard, so let's have a look at what you need to take on the big fish.

Fly Rods

Depending on how seriously you take your pike and muskie fishing, you will need an 8- to 10-weight graphite fly rod between 9 and 10 feet long. Select a rod with moderate-fast to fast action, depending on your level of casting skill. Moderate-fast rods are a little more forgiving, but trophy hunters will appreciate the extra backbone that a fast-action rod offers. You will be throwing big flies a long way for several hours, so don't compromise on rod length. A long rod will allow you to cast farther and give you more leverage when fighting big fish.

Fly Reels

Pike and muskies run hard, though typically not that far. However, they like to jump and can shake their heads like an angry bulldog. This is the middle ground where a good disc-drag fly reel is nice to have, but not necessary. You will certainly appreciate the extra line control of a disc-drag reel, and the drag allows you to put extra pressure on the fish.

A large arbor is also a good feature to have in a pike and muskie reel because it will allow you to retrieve more line with each turn. Again, this feature is not essential, but will definitely help you land trophy-size fish. If I had to choose between a disc-drag or a large-arbor reel for pike and muskies, I would go with the large arbor. Pike and muskies are not going to rocket off like bonefish, but when you get a big fish on the reel, you want to get her in as quickly as you can.

Fly Lines

Fly fishing for pike and muskies requires casting big flies a long way. You need an aggressively tapered fly line to throw these flies 60 or 70 feet. A weight-forward or shooting-head fly line is essential to making the hundreds (or thousands) of long casts required to catch a trophy pike or muskie. Many manufacturers produce specialty fly lines designed for pike and muskie fly fishing, and this can eliminate a lot of guessing as you build your rig.

A sinking-tip fly line will help you get big streamers down to pike and muskies. If you have two rod-and-reel outfits, you can keep one rigged with a sinking-tip line for swimming streamers and the other with a weight-forward floating line for surface bugs. If you only have one rod, go for a weight-forward floating line and add a sink tip with loop-to-loop connections if necessary.

Leaders

Pike and muskies have sharp teeth, and lots of them! The monofilament leaders that you use for bass and panfish will not hold up at all. Some pike and muskie anglers use heavy monofilament bite tippets, but wire tippets are even better. Choose manufactured pike and muskie leaders that have a heavy butt section and a wire bite tippet. These leaders are designed to turn over large flies and land big fish.

Flies

Whether you are fishing top-water bugs or swimming streamers, it takes big flies to catch the biggest pike and muskellunge. The term "big flies" takes on a new meaning in terms of pike and muskie fishing. Double-hook patterns featuring a pair of size 3/0 hooks are common fare for big pike and muskies. Foot-long streamers are sometimes required to tempt the biggest fish. That oversize fly-rod outfit seems a little more reasonable once you realize that you will be throwing flies that are bigger than most stocker trout.

The most popular pike and muskie flies are very similar to many bass flies. Poppers, divers, and sliders are top producing top-water bugs. Bucktail streamers are very effective for pike and muskies, as well as

No joke—when you're going after trophy pike and muskies, you'll need big streamers like this Buford, developed by Brad Bohen. KYRA PERKINSON

streamers tied with synthetic materials like FisHair and Craft Fur. As evidenced by the popularity of spinning lures, pike and muskies like a lot of flash. Be sure to stock up on flies that have plenty of Flashabou and Krystal Flash. There are many specialty flies that are designed for pike or muskies. Check out some of Brad Bohen's Musky Country Outfitters creations like the Buford or the Hang Time Optic Minnow, and you will get a good idea of the kind of flies that catch trophy pike and muskies.

Fly color is a major consideration when you tackle pike and muskies. Popular fly colors include black, orange, chartreuse, red, and white. Black is the ticket in low-light conditions or on overcast days. Pike and muskies tend to look up to feed, and black flies create a strong silhouette against gray skies. Experiment with different colors on bluebird days when the sun is high. Like bass, pike and muskie inexplicably seem to prefer one color while ignoring others.

PRESENTATIONS FOR PIKE AND MUSKIES

You can pick up a fair number of average-size pike with the same basic fly-fishing techniques used to catch largemouth and smallmouth bass. Big pike and muskies are no fools, however. If you're after trophy fish, you'll need to adjust your methods.

Long Presentations

Long casts are part of pike and muskie fly fishing. You will need to repeatedly make casts of at least 50 feet, and preferably longer. Long casts keep you from spooking fish, but there is another reason why you need to throw a lot of line for pike and muskie. Muskellunge and larger pike tend to follow flies before they strike. They frequently follow a fly several yards before striking, and will often follow the fly right up to the boat. The more distance that you put between yourself and the fly, the more opportunity you will have to elicit a strike.

Don't Stop Retrieving

There is a real temptation to slow down your retrieve when you see a pike slashing at your fly or a muskie bulging up behind it. On one hand, it makes sense that slowing your retrieve might help the fish catch your fly, but that is dead wrong. For one thing, it is probably impossible to strip a fly so fast that a pike or muskie couldn't catch it. What's more, muskellunge and pike are suspicious creatures. If you slow down your fly, they are sure to smell a rat. Whether you are fishing top-water bugs or swimming streamers, keep your fly moving no matter what happens.

The Figure Eight

If you ever watch the Sunday-morning fishing shows, you have probably seen spinning-gear anglers plunge their rod tip into the water at the end of a retrieve, stir it around, and come up with a big pike or muskie. This move is called the "figure eight," and it is designed to keep the lure moving and make a tempting final presentation to fish that have followed a lure but were reluctant to strike.

It is understandable that many fly anglers would get nervous when it comes to sticking the tip-top of an expensive fly rod underwater and swirling it around. Spinning rods aren't cheap, but fly rods are downright expensive, so use your best judgment before you make figure eights with a fly rod. There are a couple of ways that you can keep your fly moving alongside the boat without resorting to dipping your rod.

First, try sweeping your fly around the end of the boat. If you see a follow or if you suspect that a pike or muskie is keyed in on your fly, swing your rod around the end quickly so that your fly speeds up as it approaches the boat and then goes around the end. That last burst of speed can entice a wary fish to bite.

You can also jig your streamer to tempt boat-side pike and muskies. When you have retrieved your fly to the point that there are just a few feet of line in the water, raise your rod tip then lower it, allowing the fly to sink like a jig. Try this after every retrieve; you'll be surprised at how often you hook up a fish that you did not even see.

Top-Water Tactics for Pike and Muskellunge

Top-water bugs are the most exciting way to catch pike and muskies. Pike and muskies may slash at top-water flies from the side or bulge up behind your fly like a surfacing submarine. Just be sure to hold on when they strike!

The top-water bite for pike and muskellunge begins in the spring when fish are moving into warmer, shallow waters for feeding and spawning runs. Look for subsurface vegetation, shallow rocky structure, and woody cover adjacent to deeper water. Pick a target and cast your bug in as tight as you can. Make a slow, erratic retrieve by stripping line with the rod tip pointed directly at your bug. Use the two-cast technique to present your fly to deep lake-side cover as well as shallow shoreline cover.

As a general rule, calm water calls for more subtle fly action, while choppy water requires top-water bugs that cause some commotion. Use sliders when the water is smooth, and change over to more aggressive divers and poppers when the wind picks up and makes some waves. Make sure that you have a wide variety of top-water bugs so that you can match any water conditions.

Subsurface Tactics for Pike and Muskellunge

Pike and muskies will eat anything, but their main forage is other fish. Streamers are a great way to catch pike and muskies throughout the seasons and in all kinds of water conditions. The keys to successful pike and muskie streamer fishing are locating prime fish lies, making accurate casts, and presenting the streamer at the proper depth. Sink-tip fly lines and streamers with various amounts of added weight will help you get the fly in the right spot.

Look for shallow water that drops off abruptly into deeper water. Shallow areas with fresh vegetation or woody cover are great. Cast perpendicular to the cover and make a shallow presentation with your streamer. If you do not get a strike, cast to the same spot and allow your streamer to sink before retrieving. Work along the length of a weed bed or shoreline in this manner, making shallow and deep presentations to every likely spot.

Not only do pike and muskies hide in cover, they may suspend at different levels depending on water temperatures and atmospheric conditions. This two-cast approach allows you to make presentations to fish whether they are shallow or deep.

After you have worked a weed bed or shoreline in this manner, be sure to make a few presentations parallel to the cover as well. Presenting your fly along the length of a feature that you just fished will increase your catch rate. We sometimes get hung up on the idea that fish exist in a flat world, relative to the depth or line that we are fishing, but there are three dimensions to the underwater realm. Changing the angle of your presentation can make a big difference.

HOOKING AND FIGHTING PIKE AND MUSKELLUNGE

Pike and muskellunge attack their prey and kill it with big, razor-sharp teeth. However, they do not chew their food, but rather swallow it whole. When their prey is another fish, pike and muskies have to turn the fish around so that they can swallow it head first. It is very common for pike and muskies to snatch another fish, then return to their lie before turning their prey.

For anglers, this means that the first sign of a strike may not be the best time to set the hook. You should wait until you can feel the weight of the fish on your line. The weight is an indication that the fish has actually taken your fly and has either turned to swim away with it or has engulfed it. Setting the hook at the first sign of a strike can pull your fly from the fish's mouth.

Do not raise the rod tip to set the hook on a pike or muskie. When you feel the weight of the fish, strip-strike hard by pulling the fly line while your rod tip is pointed at the fish. Set the hook several times if necessary, because pike and muskies will employ every trick in the book to throw your fly, and this is only the beginning of the fight.

Once the fish is solidly hooked, you can raise the rod to apply pressure to the fish. Pike and muskies are jumpers, so be ready for a leap and be sure to keep the line tight when it happens. With a heavy leader there is little chance of a fish breaking you off. Instead, you should be more concerned with the fish throwing your fly. Keep the line tight and pressure the fish with the full flex of your fly rod.

Let the fish run if it wants to, but be sure that you don't let slack form in the line or you could get thrown. This is where a quality fly reel equipped with a disc drag comes in handy. Pike and muskellunge fight hard, but they usually don't make long runs like steelhead, carp, or bonefish. Once she has it out of her system, you should be able to recover line quickly.

LANDING AND HANDLING PIKE AND MUSKELLUNGE

Surprisingly, pike and muskellunge are delicate fish. Unlike bass, which can usually be unhooked and quickly returned to the water, pike and muskies require careful handling and must often be revived like trout before they can swim off under their own power. While small pike are plentiful in most waters, trophy-size pike and muskellunge are important natural resources that should be released whenever possible. Keeping pike and muskies alive for a trophy shot is not difficult if you handle them with care from the beginning.

You can easily handle small pike by grabbing them on the soft spots at the backs of the gill covers. This seems to pacify small pike in the same way that "lip-gripping" calms bass. Keep your hand out of the pike's gills for its sake, and stay away from its mouth for your own sake. Even small pike have plenty of teeth to send you to the emergency room.

You have probably seen anglers pick up large pike and muskies by reaching into the slot beneath the fish's jaw. I don't recommend this for a couple of reasons. First of all, sticking your hand that close to the mouth of a pike or muskie is like asking to get stitches. You might get away with it a hundred times, but sooner or later those teeth will turn on you. Second, there is too great a chance of hurting the fish when you pick it up by the jaw. You could accidentally get a finger into the gills (which can also give you a nasty cut) or even break the fish's jaw if you try to lever it up. In my opinion, it is just not worth the risk of getting hurt or hurting the fish. Get a large net or a cradle net to land larger pike and muskies.

You should have jaw spreaders, side-cut pliers, and some tool for extracting deep-hooked flies. Jaw spreaders make the task of removing hooks much easier and safer. Long hemostats, needle-nose pliers, and commercial hook extractors will all serve the purpose of removing your fly from the gullet of a pike or muskie. De-barbing your fly hooks will make the task much easier. If you encounter a difficult situation where you cannot get the fly out without hurting the fish, use your side-cut pliers to cut off the fly so that you can get the fish back in the water.

Pike and muskellunge often need to be revived before they can be returned to the water. Don't just toss a fish back in the water; it might not survive. Cradle pike and muskie under the belly and hold them by the tail so that you can revive them by gently moving them back and forth in the water. Wait until the fish is able to swim away on its own.

PIKE AND MUSKELLUNGE CONSERVATION

Pike are good eating fish, but be responsible if you harvest any pike for the frying pan. A couple of small pike will feed most families, so there is no need to go overboard keeping fish. Catching a big pike on a fly rod is a major fly-fishing accomplishment. Treat large pike with care, and keep only a photo or two so that you can remember your trophy.

As apex predators, muskellunge are not nearly as numerous as pike. Years of catch-and-keep practices as well as pressure from spear-fishing and habitat degradation have added to the stress felt by muskies. Even where it is legal to keep a muskie, I recommend releasing every one that you catch so that future generations can share in the excitement of fly fishing for these legendary gamefish.

PIKE AND MUSKELLUNGE FLIES

Buford

Hook: Daiichi 2546 or equivalent big-game
Thread: Ultra Thread 210 Denier
Tail: Bucktail
Flash: Krystal Flash
Kicker legs: Webby rooster hackle
Long hackles: Whiting Farms genetic hackle
Collar: Bucktail
Head: Clipped ends of bucktail collar
Note: This Brad Bohen creation looks a bit unwieldy, but the bucktail and hackles create a good deal of bulk with a surprisingly small amount of material.

Whistler

Hook: Daiichi 2546 or equivalent big-game
Thread: Ultra Thread 210 Denier
Eyes: Bead chain
Tail: Bucktail
Flash: Flashabou
Kicker legs: Rooster saddle hackle
Hackle: Webby rooster saddle hackle
Note: Going pike fishing without a red-and-white Whistler is like going trout fishing without an Adams.

Dahlberg Mega Diver

Hook: Mustad C52S BLN or equivalent stinger

Thread: Ultra Thread 210 Denier

Weed guard: 30-pound monofilament

Tail: Hackle feathers, bucktail, Flashabou, or synthetic hair

Body: Spun-and-clipped deer hair

Eyes: Plastic doll eyes, attached with Goop

Note: Tie in a nice clump of bucktail when you start the tail of a Mega Diver, then keep the flash and synthetic material sparse. The bucktail will help prevent fouling.

CHAPTER 8

Stripers and Temperate Bass

If you're like most of us, you probably suffer from a case of "the grass is always greener" when you read about the exotic sport fish that haunt far-off fly-fishing destinations. For many warmwater anglers, a trip to the salt to chase sea-going gamefish is out of the question. But what would you say if I told you that you can catch big, aggressive saltwater gamefish in many large freshwater reservoirs around the United States? It sounds too good to be true, but in fact striped bass have been stocked and allowed to reproduce in a large number of highland reservoirs for over fifty years.

Stripers are the anadromous cousins of the more familiar white bass. Both are members of the temperate bass family and exhibit behaviors and characteristics different from the common "black" bass. White bass are strictly freshwater fish, frequently found in lakes and big rivers. However, the native habitat of the striped bass is most of the eastern seaboard of the United States, where the fish would feed throughout the year at sea before running up freshwater rivers to spawn. Striped bass were trapped during the construction of Santee Cooper Reservoir in South Carolina in the 1940s. Although biologists believed that the fish would die off without access to saltwater, it was determined that the species could not only survive but actually thrive in freshwater.

Today striped bass have been introduced to many large reservoirs across the United States, where they often live alongside the native white bass. Some natural reproduction of stripers takes place in the wild, though many reservoirs lack access to suitable spawning grounds and must be stocked. In order to control populations, some reservoirs are stocked with hybrid striped bass, also known as "wipers." Wipers are the sterile, hatchery-raised progeny of stripers and white bass.

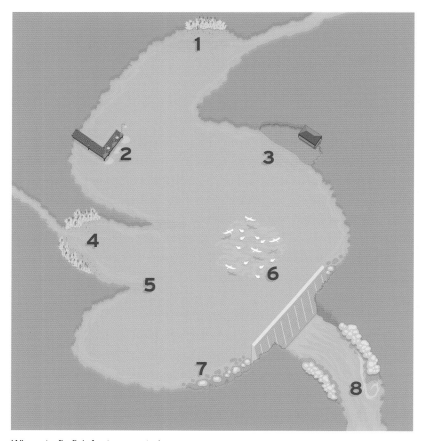

Where to fly fish for temperate bass:

1. Shallow, sandy creek bays

2. Docks and piers with lights (early-morning and late-night striper hot spot)

3. Swimming beach

4. Deep creek arms

5. Points off of creek arms

6. School of baitfish breaking the surface (look for boiling water and circling birds)

7. Riprap-lined banks

8. Rocky outcroppings below large dams

STRIPERS, WIPERS, AND WHITE BASS—WHAT'S THE DIFFERENCE?

Striped bass, white bass, and hybrid wipers exhibit very similar behaviors in freshwater. All three are open-water predators that feed primarily on baitfish, and all three are schooling fish that feed aggressively in packs. Stripers, wipers, and white bass attack schools of baitfish, which gather into tight balls to evade the predators. The baitfish often move higher in the water column and may even jump out of the water in an attempt to escape temperate bass. Jumping baitfish are a good clue that there are stripers, wipers, or white bass nearby.

Size is the major difference between striped bass, white bass, and hybrid wipers. White bass are the smallest of the three, usually averaging about 1½ or 2 pounds. Striped bass are much larger, with trophy-size fish weighing in at 30 pounds or more. As you might expect, hybrid wipers fall somewhere in between. White bass are shaped more like large crappies, with flat pan-shaped bodies. Striped bass are sleek, torpedo-shaped fish, while hybrid wipers again show traits of both species. White bass are striped, though stripers feature darker lines on their flanks. Hybrid wipers have irregular, broken lines along their sides.

Because of the difference in size, you will need progressively heavier tackle when fishing for white bass, hybrid wipers, and striped bass. However, the habits and habitats of the three species are similar enough that we can look at the group as a whole when considering angling tactics and techniques.

SEASONAL MOVEMENTS AND PRIME LOCATIONS

The movements of temperate bass in a reservoir or river are primarily determined by one simple factor: the location of the baitfish. Finding baitfish will put you onto temperate bass in a hurry. Of course, locating baitfish is sometimes easier said than done. Let's consider how baitfish movement and other factors during the seasons affect the location and availability of temperate bass.

Striped bass like this will test your tackle and angling skills.
HENRY COWEN

Spring

Springtime temperate bass move into shallow waters like creek arms and coves because these areas tend to warm more quickly than other parts of a lake or river system. The warm water attracts baitfish, which draws gamefish. Temperate bass can be found in the spring feeding on baitfish in the shallows or staged in deeper water adjacent to a shallow feeding ground. This is the time of year when temperate bass make feeding runs up creek arms, into shallow coves, and onto sandy swimming beaches because that is where the baitfish are concentrated.

The need to feed is not the only urge driving stripers and white bass in the spring. The fish move into creek arms or upstream on main rivers to spawn when water temperatures reach the mid-50s. Look for runs of stripers and white bass moving into the shallows in reservoirs. You will find male stripers suspended on points along the main lake, while females move into the creek arms to gorge on baitfish. Stripers and white bass may also run up the main river at the head of the reservoir if it is accessible.

Stripers and white bass that live in river systems run upstream, holding in deep pools until they reach a barrier such as a dam. That is where they will spawn before moving back downstream. Temperate bass fishing, especially for white bass below a dam, can be fast and furious when a spawning run is on.

Reservoir-dwelling temperate bass move out of the creek arms after spawning and continue to pattern their movements after the baitfish. Late-spring and early-summer temperate bass may spend the majority of their days in open water, but they make frequent feeding runs into the same coves and creek arms in which they fed earlier in the year. Look early in the morning and late in the evening for temperate bass that are feeding in the shallows. During the day you can also find them suspended off points adjacent to the feeding grounds.

Summer

Rising summer water temperatures cause temperate bass to retreat to the thermocline, which is basically the depth of a lake or reservoir at which the water stays cool during the summer. Locating the thermocline is a very important part of bait-fishing and trolling for temperate bass because the fish can reliably be found there throughout the summer. Of course, bait-fishing and trolling gear can easily reach the thermocline, which is often at 30 feet or deeper. The average fly angler will have to go to a lot of trouble to fish that kind of depth, and there is no guarantee of success. Rather than probe the depths with fly gear, look for favorable conditions that bring temperate bass closer to the surface.

Summer fly fishing for stripers, wipers, and white bass can be dynamite on cloudy, overcast days and when weather fronts are moving through your area. These conditions bring baitfish as well as temperate bass higher in the water column, often resulting in extended periods of temperate bass feeding at or near the surface. Look for telltale signs of activity such as baitfish busting above the surface or birds circling above the water.

Don't count out those familiar shallow areas like coves, creek arms, and swimming beaches during the summer either. You will need to adjust your sleeping schedule a bit, as the fish are more likely to hit the shallows late at night or early in the morning. Try hitting the water an hour or two earlier so that you can look for bass in the shallows before launching your boat.

Autumn

As cool fall weather moves in, temperate bass move higher in the water column. They will also begin to use shallow creek arms and coves more frequently for feeding. In addition to open-water feeding blitzes, be on the lookout for temperate bass moving into the shallows and staging along points on the reservoir. Keep a sharp eye on changing water temperatures, atmospheric conditions, and baitfish movements, and you will catch fish well into winter.

Winter

Winter finds stripers, wipers, and white bass once again looking to either the depths or the shallowest water for baitfish. Fly rodders might as well forget about fishing the deepest water for bass, but a couple of sunny days can warm the shallows enough to draw baitfish and bass into those familiar old coves and creek arms.

Stripers under the Lights

If you really want to see some bass in action, check out the sport going on under a dock light during the spring, summer, or early fall. Baitfish are attracted to the light, and you can bet that the bass are not far behind. Observing the bass as they slash through the baitfish will give you a

Striped bass guide Henry Cowen with one of his close friends. HENRY COWEN

greater appreciation for the way that these predators feed. Of course, tossing a fly into the fray is probably the most guaranteed hookup in the entire fishing world. Find a dock with dusk-to-dawn lights or install a light on your own dock and enjoy the show!

FLY-FISHING GEAR FOR STRIPERS, WIPERS, AND WHITE BASS

Temperate bass vary greatly in size depending on the species and their environments. It is important to match your fly-fishing equipment to the size of fish that you are likely to encounter. Crappie-size white bass can certainly be landed on heavy fly tackle, but the sport loses its allure when you can simply lift the fish from the water with a 10-weight rod. On the other hand, throwing large weighted Clouser Minnows with a 5-weight fly rod is an exercise in futility, not to mention the short work a 30-pound striper will make of your trout gear if you manage to get hooked up.

Fly Rods

A 5- or 6-weight fly rod is sufficient for white bass. A 9-foot or longer rod will allow you to make longer casts. Choose a graphite rod with moderate-fast to fast action so that you can throw large streamers.

Striped bass and hybrid wipers call for heavier tackle. Begin building your striper outfit with an 8- to 10-weight graphite rod at least 9 feet long. A rod with moderate-fast action is the best choice for throwing big streamers with a floating or intermediate fly line. If you already have a good moderate-fast fly rod, consider adding a 10-weight graphite rod with slower action to your arsenal. Fly fishing for stripers often requires casting a full-sink fly line. A slow-action fly rod can make it easier to pick up a lot of sunken line.

Fly Lines

You will need to make a lot of long casts to catch stripers, wipers, and striped bass. A weight-forward or bass-bug-taper floating fly line is best for casting top-water bugs or presenting swimming streamers just below the surface. Oversizing your fly line by one or two weights is a good idea if you are a weak fly caster. A shooting-head fly line is another good choice if you have trouble throwing large streamers and bugs.

An intermediate-sinking fly line will help you present streamers in the middle depths. The intermediate line is likely to be your go-to fly line for much of your striper fishing, so don't skimp on this one. Be sure to select a fly line that is rated for your rod when choosing an intermediate-sinking line. These lines are quite heavy and cast easily compared to floating fly lines. Oversizing a sinking fly line can actually hurt your ability to cast the line and may damage your fly rod.

For stripers, wipers, and white bass that are holding deep along ridges and points, you will need a full-sinking fly line. These lines are uniformly weighted so that they sink at a predetermined rate. You can even get non-weighted streamers down in a hurry when using a full-sinking fly line. Here again, be sure that you match up your full-sinking fly line to your fly rod.

Because temperate bass are schooling fish and feed in packs, the action can be fast when you get into fish. You should be ready to make any presentation that is required at a moment's notice. It may not be practical to invest in three entire fly-fishing outfits, but you will be a step ahead of the game if you have three rods rigged up at all times. A floating-line outfit with a top-water bug, an intermediate-sinking outfit with a streamer, and a full-sinking outfit with a streamer will cover any situation and you will not have to fumble with spare reel-spools while the fish are biting. Do your research and compare prices of some lesser-known manufacturers. Spend a little more for the fly line and less on the rod and reel. I have put together some bulletproof outfits for less than some folks pay for a reel, and you can, too!

Reels

A run-of-the-mill reel with a clicker-style drag will work fine for white bass fly fishing. You probably will not even need (or want) to get a white bass on the reel because they are fairly easy to land and reeling in the line is wasted fishing time.

Striped bass and hybrid wipers are another story. It is very likely that you will have to deal with at least one strong run when you hook into a striper or hybrid. This is when a large-arbor reel with a disc-drag system can really make a difference. When stripers run away from you, the disc drag will increase the pressure on the fish, wearing it out more quickly. Stripers might also run right at you faster than you can reel in the line. If that is the case, you will appreciate a large-arbor reel so that you can pick up the mess once you have your fish under control.

Again, I don't recommend a top-of-the-line reel if you are just starting out. Skill and patience will allow you to land some pretty nice fish with modest equipment. However, if it is trophies that you seek, do not go cheap when selecting a reel for striped bass fly fishing.

Leaders

You will probably not need to use complex saltwater-style leaders for stripers in freshwater, but don't use a trout leader either. A tapered knotless monofilament leader with a stiff butt will cast large flies easily and allow you to present them to fish near the surface. You can purchase manufactured knotless monofilament leaders that are designed for use in striped bass fly fishing and work beautifully. Use a heavy fluorocarbon leader for subsurface presentations made with a sinking line, especially if you are fishing around rocky points.

Flies

Temperate bass are primarily fish-eaters, so the flies that you use to catch them should match the type of forage fish in your reservoir or river. Gizzard shad and threadfin shad are the most common baitfish that bass key on. Blueback herring and alewives are the primary baitfish in some waters, so be sure to match the size and color of the baitfish where you are fishing.

Top-water offerings such as poppers, sliders, divers, and Live Body foam flies are a great choice when stripers, wipers, and white bass are busting bait on surface. Try to match the approximate size and color of the baitfish that bass are feeding on, but don't get hung up on "matching the hatch" during a feeding frenzy. Just get a reasonable facsimile of the baitfish into the fray and hang on!

When temperate bass are not feeding on top, you will need to present streamers that imitate the local forage. Saltwater-style streamers are the norm for subsurface stripers. This may be due to their saltwater roots, or just because they work. Clouser Minnows, Deceivers, Cowen's Baitfish, Whitlock's Sheep Hair Shad, and Keliher's Juve are top baitfish patterns. Cowen's Coyote deserves a special spot in your streamer box as well. It is a Clouser-style fly that includes a small swivel and a blade, making it an excellent attractor pattern for all occasions.

The same flies will catch hybrid wipers and white bass. You may want to tie these flies in smaller sizes for white bass, as they are not nearly as large as stripers. However, don't doubt that any of these game-fish can take a large fly.

Other Equipment

A stripping basket is standard fare for saltwater anglers chasing stripers. It is simply an open basket, attached to your waist by a belt, which you can strip fly line into while fishing. You will need to make many long casts when fly fishing for temperate bass. You can strip line into the basket so that it does not become a tangled mess around your legs or get damaged underfoot.

You should keep a pair of binoculars handy when fishing for temperate bass on large reservoirs. When bass start busting baitfish on the surface, you need to get there in a hurry. Binoculars will help you pick up on telltale signs of surface activity such as boiling water and circling birds.

A plastic tackle organizer will keep your big flies organized for a day of fishing for temperate bass. KYRA PERKINSON

PRESENTATIONS FOR STRIPERS, WIPERS, AND WHITE BASS

Top-Water Presentations

Temperate bass are aggressive pack feeders and will snap up a well-placed fly in a split second. You don't need to get too scientific when fish are feeding heavily, but there are some techniques that will help you get more hookups with bigger fish.

When you are fishing top-water bugs to feeding fish, throw your fly right into the mix for an instant hookup. You won't need to impart much action other than the standard pop-and-pause retrieve. Temperate bass that are feeding aggressively will often snatch your fly as soon as it hits the water.

You can also use top-water bugs to search out temperate bass on tailraces below large dams. Temperate bass run upstream and hold in the fast water below the dam, which concentrates a lot of bass in a relatively small space. When bass are actively feeding in the tailrace, you can cast right into the feeding frenzy. Make long casts from the shore and use the pop-and-pause retrieve to draw bass to the surface when there is no apparent feeding activity. Shad and other baitfish are frequently drawn through dams, emerging as stunned and easy prey for hungry bass waiting in the tailrace. Retrieving a Live Body popper with intermittent jerks is a good way to imitate a stunned shad and will lead to a lot of hookups on your local tailrace.

Subsurface Presentations

Temperate bass do not always feed on the surface. Subsurface presentations can be more effective depending on the water temperature, atmospheric conditions, and the amount of light on the water. Your streamers should be tied in various weights, from non-weighted baitfish patterns to heavily weighted Clouser Deep Minnows. When combined with an intermediate or full-sinking fly line, these flies will allow you to make presentations at any depth.

As is the case with top-water flies, a streamer tossed into the midst of a feeding frenzy will get snapped up in a hurry as long as it reasonably

141

resembles the baitfish. When temperate bass are feeding aggressively, just get your fly in there for fast action.

When bass are present but not aggressively feeding, you need to add a little action to entice a take. Weighted swimming streamers like Clouser Minnows, Cowen's Baitfish, and Half-and-Half flies have great baitfish action because they sink when you are not stripping line. Retrieving these flies with a steady series of line strips will result in a presentation that looks a lot like a struggling baitfish working its way through the water.

Use this combination of a weighted swimming-streamer and a steady retrieve to search for bass in shallow coves and creek arms on reservoirs. You can also use this technique in tailraces and further downstream where temperate bass hide in deep bends and pools.

Combine a heavy streamer with a full-sinking fly line to search deeper structure such as deep points near the creek arms where spawning bass are staged. Remember that the bass will move into the shallows to feed when baitfish are present, but they will also hold along the rocky points when feeding in the shallows is slow. Use your full-sinking line and heavy streamer to search along the length and depth of the point, just like you would for cool-weather black bass.

You can use the same retrieve to fish non-weighted streamers when temperate bass are feeding on baitfish in shallow water. Non-weighted streamers sink much slower and allow you to make your presentation just beneath the surface when you use a floating fly line. Using a non-weighted streamer (or even a floating top-water fly) with a sinking fly line will present bottom-hugging bass with a tempting baitfish pattern that is suspended just off the bottom. This technique can be deadly on cold-weather bass of all stripes.

The Two-Hand Retrieve

Spinning-gear anglers have always held a major advantage over fly anglers in that they can retrieve a lure as steadily and quickly as they can turn the reel. Sometimes that speedy presentation is what turns bass on, but how can you make a quick and steady retrieve when you are stripping line?

There is an old saltwater trick that will let you retrieve your bass flies quickly and steadily, just like the spinning-gear crowd. Make a long cast and tuck the butt of your fly rod, along with the reel, under your left arm (or your right arm if you are a left-handed angler). Now hold the reel tight in your armpit and retrieve line with *both* hands. You can make a fast and steady retrieve in this manner, working the fly line in hand-over-hand. When you get a strike, just set the hook with a firm line strip, hold it steady with your left hand, and get your rod out with your right hand. Now you are ready for battle with the rod in your right hand, the line in your left hand, and a bass on the fly.

CATCHING, FIGHTING, AND HANDLING STRIPERS, WIPERS, AND WHITE BASS

Hooking and Fighting Temperate Bass

Stripers, wipers, and white bass that are pack-feeding take flies in a hurry. Set the hook hard when you feel the weight of the fish with a solid strip-strike. If you are catching white bass or small hybrids, you can strip the fish right in. This will save a lot of time when you are fishing to pack-feeding bass because you don't have to feed out line and false-cast to get your fly back in the water once your fish is unhooked.

When you are fishing stripers, you should get the fish on the reel if possible. Big stripers can run hard, and any pressure that you can apply with the rod and reel will be to your advantage as well as the well-being of the fish. Get a striper on the reel and fight it with reel-drag until the fish stops running. Let your gear wear out the fish and be patient. If the bass wants to run, let it because you will only end up busting your leader or tearing out the hook if you try to wrestle a striper into the net. Don't be surprised if it takes several minutes to land a decent-size striper.

Tips for Fast-Action Bass Fishing

Stripers, wipers, and white bass are schooling fish. When they attack a school of baitfish, the action can be very fast. You can reasonably expect a hookup on every cast when you are fishing a top-water feeding frenzy, so put the odds in your favor to maximize your catch.

If you do not do it already, you should de-barb your hooks when fishing for temperate bass. Fishing barbless hooks is the number-one way that you can increase the survival rate of fish that you release. De-barbed hooks penetrate deeper and are much easier to remove once you have landed the fish. When bass are busting the surface all around you, the last thing that you want to worry about is digging a barbed hook out of your fish.

You should be familiar enough with the forage fish in your local waters that you can reasonably imitate them with flies. Temperate bass are not really selective when pack-feeding, but you will catch more fish if you can match the general size and color of the baitfish that they are keying on.

Be sure to keep at least two fly rods rigged for every angler. Not only will this help you cover different fishing conditions, but you will also appreciate the extra rod when you break off a fish or lose a fly. Once again, when the water is boiling with bass, you won't want to mess with tying on a new leader or changing out a fly.

Handling Stripers, Wipers, and White Bass
Temperate bass have small, harmless teeth. You can grip temperate bass by the lower lip with your thumb and forefinger just like you would a black bass. When the bass is within reach, just grab the leader and slide your hand down to the fish and grab it by the lip.

Temperate bass can be handled by the lip, just like black bass.
HENRY COWEN

If you are releasing the fish and don't want to take a photo, you should try to remove the hook without taking the bass from the water. This puts less stress on the bass and increases the survival rate of released fish. If you want to remove your bass from the water, be sure to hold it vertically by the lip and support the fish's body with your other hand if you turn it horizontally.

You will probably want a landing net when fishing for stripers and big hybrids. These fish cannot hurt you like a pike or muskellunge, but they can be a bit unruly and a net will ensure that you get your trophy into the boat for a couple of photos.

Catch-and-Release

Keeping temperate bass raises a couple of ethical questions. They are schooling fish, so there is a perception that they are much more numerous than black bass, pike, and muskellunge. In addition, striped bass and wipers are usually stocked fish, which leads to a "put-and-take" mentality among some anglers.

I am not completely against keeping a few fish, but I don't think that fishing for freezer meat or for trophy mounts is the best way to ensure great fishing down the road. Keep a few small fish if you like, but return the real trophy fish to the water so that they can be enjoyed again and again.

Handle trophy stripers carefully and release them so that they can fight another day. HENRY COWEN

145

TEMPERATE BASS FLIES

Lefty's Deceiver

Hook: Mustad S71SZ-34007 or equivalent big-game
Thread: Danville's Flymaster 70 Denier
Tail: Six hackle feathers
Belly: White bucktail
Flash: Krystal Flash
Sides: White bucktail
Top: Gray bucktail
Eyes: Stick-on eyes, attached with Goop

Synthetic Hair Baitfish

Hook: Mustad S71SZ-34007 or equivalent big-game
Thread: Danville's Flymaster 70 Denier
Tail, body, and back: Synthetic hair such as EP Fibers or Farrar's Flash Blend
Flash: Pearl Flashabou
Belly: White Craft Fur
Head: Prismatic stick-on eyes coated with 5-minute epoxy
Note: Add varying amounts of non-lead wire to this pattern before you tie in the synthetic hair to fish the pattern at different depths.

Foam-Head Baitfish

Hook: Mustad S71SZ-34007 or equivalent big-game
Thread: Danville's Flymaster 70 Denier
Tail: Synthetic hair and ostrich herl
Head: Craft foam, cut to shape and hot-glued to hook

Juve Fly

Hook: Mustad S71SZ-34007 or equivalent big-game
Thread: Danville's Flymaster 70 Denier
Belly: White bucktail
Back: Dark bucktail
Head: Prismatic stick-on eyes coated with 5-minute epoxy

Cowen's Coyote

Hook: Mustad S71SZ-34007 or equivalent big-game
Thread: Ultra Thread 210 Denier
Eyes: Lead dumbbell eyes
Belly: White bucktail
Flash: Flashabou
Wing: Dark bucktail
Spinner: Size 0 spinner with barrel swivel and split-ring
Head: 5-minute epoxy
Note: To tie this fly, I slide one-half of the barrel swivel over the hook eye and epoxy it in place when I finish the head.

Blueback Crease Fly

Hook: Mustad R75-79580 or equivalent streamer
Thread: Danville's Flymaster 70 Denier
Tail: Hackle feathers
Flash: Krystal Flash
Body: Craft foam, cut to shape and hot-glued to the hook shank
Eyes: Stick-on prismatic eyes
Coating: 5-minute epoxy
Note: Here again, feel free to go wild with the Sharpie markers and make this fly work for you!

Live Body Popper

Hook: Mustad C52S BLN or equivalent stinger

Thread: Danville's Flymaster 70 Denier

Tail: Bucktail

Flash: Krystal Flash

Hackle: Rooster hackle

Body: Live Foam Popper Body or equivalent

Eyes: Stick-on prismatic eyes

Coating: 5-minute epoxy

CHAPTER 9

Fly Fishing for Carp

Carp may be different things to different people. To some folks they are a nuisance fish that gobbles up gamefish eggs and destroys prime fishing habitats (neither of which is true, by the way). To others, particularly those outside of the United States, they are an important source of food. In some places, such as the runoff-rich environments of golf courses and industrial parks, carp provide cheap landscape labor as living aquatic weed-whackers. Of course, the most common perception among anglers is that carp are simply trash fish that sometimes wind up on our lines through some unfortunate alignment of the fly-fishing universe. Nothing could be further from the truth.

If you have ever hooked a carp, you know that they run farther and fight harder than nearly any other freshwater gamefish. If you actually landed that carp, you know that carp can reach enormous sizes in even the most marginal environments. And if you have actually fly fished for carp, you know that they are the most skittish fish in freshwater.

The common carp is a result of hundreds of years of breeding that has produced the fish we know today. Carp are omnivorous, meaning that they eat both plant and animal material. They can survive a wide range of water temperatures from near-freezing to over 100°F. They thrive in crystal-clear lakes and murky, silt-laden rivers. Carp make use of their excellent senses of smell, touch, and hearing to find food and to avoid predators. They form loose packs, called shoals, and react to danger by emitting warning pheromones that scatter the shoal and keep fish away from the area for hours or days. This all adds up to one challenging gamefish!

WHERE DO CARP LIVE?

Carp can live in nearly any lake, pond, creek, or river as long as there is sufficient forage. Keep in mind that sufficient forage can include plant material as far as carp are concerned, so carp territory really covers a wide range of environments.

Consider the following example: The rocky flats of northeastern Lake Michigan are considered some of the best carp-fishing waters in the Midwest. The White River in downtown Indianapolis is another excellent place to catch trophy-size carp. The White River, which has suffered its share of industrial pollution and fish kills, is a far cry from the crystal waters of the northern Lake Michigan flats. However, due to the adaptability of carp, you can catch plenty of big fish in both places.

Some of the more unusual places that you will find carp are the retention ponds in apartment complexes or industrial parks. They are also commonly found in golf course ponds, where grass carp and common carp are stocked to keep down weed growth. The good news is that carp are abundant enough that there are probably great opportunities for a shot at trophy carp right in your neighborhood.

UNDERSTANDING CARP MOVEMENTS AND LOCATING FISH

Like other fish, carp are found where there is food. Because of their expanded menus, that means that carp can be found just about anywhere in a body of water at some time. However, understanding how water temperature and depth affect the emergence of the carp's favorite food sources will help you narrow down your search.

Your best shot at carp is most likely to be when the fish are feeding in rocky shallows or in shallow mudflats. These usually occur near the

Sight fishing for carp is a lot like fly fishing for bonefish. HENRY COWEN

banks of a lake or on the backwaters of lakes and streams. Shallow water receives more sunlight than deep water, allowing dense plant growth to occur. Shallow water also warms up more quickly than deep water, encouraging the emergence of aquatic insects and invertebrates. These organisms thrive on the substrate provided by aquatic plants, and the presence of insects and invertebrates attracts baitfish. Rocky shallows are favored by crayfish, stoneflies, and hellgrammites, while nutrient-rich mudflats hold vast numbers of mollusks, snails, leeches, and aquatic worms. This all adds up to a whole lot of carp food in shallow water.

Carp that are feeding in rocky shallows or mudflats are often said to be "tailing." If you are familiar with saltwater fly fishing, you have probably heard this term used by anglers seeking bonefish or redfish. Like these saltwater gamefish, carp frequently feed with their heads down, vacuuming food from the bottom or rooting up mud to dislodge buried food. When carp tip their noses down in shallow water, their tails break the surface. If you see carp tails peeking above the surface, you are only a cast away from actively feeding carp.

As you become more attuned to the movements of carp, you will notice that fish frequently cruise along the shallows and over the edges where shallow water drops off into deeper water. Carp move from one shallow feeding area to another via deep water, so there is a good chance that the fish are in the mood to feed if you can see them moving into a

151

shallow area. A well-placed fly in front of cruising carp is a great way to hook up with opportunistic fish looking for a quick meal.

Due to their omnivorous nature, carp key on many different types of food as they become available. One of the more unusual sources of carp nutrition is floating fruits and seeds. Mulberries and tree seeds such as cottonwood and maple seeds attract the attention of carp, so keep an eye out for surface-feeding carp that are taking advantage of windfall fruit.

Carp will also feed on the surface when there are heavy insect hatches or spinner falls. Carp really tend to favor spent insects as they gather in scum lines along banks or current seams. Even if you don't see the insects, carp cruising just under the surface with their mouths breaking the water are a dead giveaway that there is something to eat on the surface.

There are also a couple of situations that you would do well to avoid when fly fishing for carp. When you encounter a group of carp that are loafing in the sun, often with their backs above the surface, forget about them. Carp love to soak up the sun, and it is next to impossible to coax them into taking a fly when they are sunbathing.

Likewise, you should avoid spawning carp. You will know spawning fish when you see them because they will be crawling over each other, digging up a lot of mud, coming out of the water, and generally having a rowdy time. It is pretty tempting to toss your fly into the fray, but your effort will most likely be in vain.

Carp have thick lips and large, downward-pointing mouths. HENRY COWEN

FLY-FISHING EQUIPMENT FOR CARP

Carp are big fish capable of long, powerful runs. While you might be casting tiny nymphs, dry flies, and small streamers to carp, you will need some heavy equipment to handle the fish once you have it hooked.

Fly Rods

Select an 8-weight, 9-foot graphite fly rod with moderate-fast action for carp fishing. You will need an 8-weight to tire the fish and to control them as you are trying to bring them to the net. A 9-foot rod will allow you to make longer casts and throw longer, lighter leaders than would be feasible with a shorter fly rod.

Carp are very perceptive and will pick up on the slightest hint of lurking danger. If you are going to get serious about fly fishing for carp, select a fly rod that has a subdued color scheme and no flashy hardware. Shiny new fly rods are great, but there is also a chance of putting down an entire shoal of tailing carp if the sun catches your rod just right.

Fly Lines

Subdued colors are the best choice for fly lines as well. Choose a weight-forward floating fly line that matches the rated weight of your fly rod. You won't be throwing supersized flies for carp, so there is really no reason to size up your line.

Reel and Backing

A Great Lakes steelhead can seem downright lazy compared to the mile-long runs that carp can take you on. You can land carp with a cheap clicker-drag reel, but it will be much easier if you invest in a large-arbor reel with a disc drag. The disc drag will keep your line in order when a carp runs, and you can dial the drag in to put extra pressure on the fish.

If you have never seen the backing on your reel, the first carp you hook is likely to show it to you. Load your reel with as much 20- or 30-pound Dacron backing as you can. You will need it.

Leaders

Under normal circumstances you can use an 8- or 9-foot knotless leader for carp fishing. In gin-clear water and when fishing to spooky carp, you will have to put a little more distance between your fly line and the fly, so pack along a few spools of 3X or 4X tippet material as well.

Carp tend to hang out in weedy, algae-laden waters, so use knotless leaders to reduce the amount of goop you have to clean off your line. Fluorocarbon is great because it keeps light flies from hanging up in the surface, is resistant to abrasion, and is nearly invisible underwater. Keep a few monofilament leaders handy as well, for those times when you have an opportunity to take carp on top-water flies.

Other Equipment

Small carp are easy enough to handle, but you will want a net to land large fish. A big, long-handled net will make the job much easier.

You will also need a pair of needle-nose pliers or hemostats to remove hooks. Carp have thick, leathery lips that really hold hooks. Of course, de-barbing your fly hooks will help as well.

Sight fishing is the most successful technique used to catch carp on a fly rod. Polarized sunglasses are an essential part of any carp fly-fishing outfit. Without polarized sunglasses you are guaranteed to miss

Early morning with still water is the perfect time to fly fish for carp. HENRY COWEN

a dozen carp for every one that you spot. Put simply, if you forget your polarized specs, you might as well have forgotten your fly rod.

CARP FLIES

Given the wide variety of food that carp will eat, it should come as no surprise that there are all kinds of carp flies out there. I like to break them down into four categories: dry flies, nymphs, swimming streamers, and bottom streamers. Let's have a look at some examples of each type.

Dry Flies

This category includes flies that imitate special carp foods, such as mulberry fruit and cottonwood seeds, as well as traditional dry flies that imitate top-water insects, like mayflies and caddis. Carp may rise to a specific object, but surface-feeding carp often simply skim objects from the surface like a vacuum cleaner. Accurate placement of dry flies that mimic the overall size, shape, and color of the food carp are taking will trump "match the hatch" dry-fly fishing in most cases.

Nymphs

Insect nymphs, larvae, and pupae make up a good percentage of carp food day in and day out. Whether the carp are tailing in mudflats for buried food or cruising in search of a quick snack, sight-casting nymphs is probably the most effective technique for catching carp on the fly. You don't need to spend hours at the fly-tying vise churning out anatomically precise nymph replicas, however. The same nondescript searching patterns that catch trout work great for carp. Fill a fly box with plenty of Gold-Ribbed Hare's Ears, Whitlock's Red Fox Squirrel Nymphs, Clouser's Swimming Nymphs, and Prince Nymphs to cover all of the smaller-size insect life in your local carp water. Throw in an assortment of olive, brown, and black Woolly Worms and Woolly Buggers in sizes 6 through 10 to cover larger nymphs such as stoneflies, dragonflies, damselflies, and hellgrammites. Be sure to tie your nymphs in various weights so that you can easily get the fly down to feeding carp in shallow water as well as deeper water.

Swimming Streamers

Carp feed on baitfish in shallow and deep water as well. While you may encounter carp slashing at a school of baitfish in open water, your best chances of hooking carp on a swimming streamer will be in the rocky shallows and mudflats. Lighter versions of popular swimming streamers like the Clouser Minnow and the Half-and-Half tied with bead-chain eyes will sink slower. Non-weighted swimming streamers like Whitlock's Sheep Hair Shad are a good choice when carp are feeding on baitfish in very shallow water.

Bottom Streamers

Crayfish are a favorite choice for hungry carp, so it makes sense to imitate these common crustaceans. Again, there is no need for precise imitation. Size, color, and action are the most important factors. Tie patterns such as Whitlock's Near 'Nuff Crayfish, Holschlag's Hackle Fly, Clouser's Foxee Minnow, and my Skittish Crayfish in various weights.

Carp also feed on bottom-dwelling baitfish like sculpins and madtoms. Whitlock's Near 'Nuff Sculpin is a great choice, along with weighted Muddler Minnow variations in darker colors. Be sure to systematically add weight to your bottom streamers so that you know how quickly they will reach the bottom in water of different depths.

Bonefish-style flies like Crazy Charlies make good carp flies, too. They are relatively snag-proof; can be tied in a variety of sizes, weights, and colors; and imitate all kinds of foods that carp like.

APPROACHING CARP

Carp are exceptionally wary fish that will surprise even the most ardent tailwater trout-anglers with their spooky dispositions. Once you have spotted feeding carp, you need to get yourself within casting distance. Your best bet is to stay out of the water altogether if you can. Because carp frequently feed in shallows, it is pretty easy to spot and approach fish from the bank.

Of course, there are times when you will have to wade in order to get within striking distance. Go slow and stay low to avoid spooking the fish. Try to approach the fish from a direction that provides a background, such as a tree line, so that the fish cannot make out your silhouette against the sky.

If you are casting to a shoal of feeding carp, study the fish for a moment and determine which fish you can most likely make a presentation to without spooking the others. This will almost always be a fish on the edge of the shoal nearest to you. Don't get greedy and cast right into the middle of the shoal because your line will spook any fish that it falls over, and one spooked carp will put the entire shoal down.

Do not false cast over the carp. Even the shadow of your line is enough to send carp scurrying off to deep water. Keep a length of fly line out and hold your fly like a saltwater angler searching for bonefish from a boat. Your first cast represents your best shot at a hookup, so make it count. Every cast to feeding carp should be well planned. Even if your cast is off-target, let it lie and fish it out because you will spook the carp if you rip the line off the water to make another cast. If you must false cast, do it far off to the side, then direct your presentation cast toward the fish.

PRESENTING FLIES TO CARP

You have probably gathered that catching carp on the fly requires a stealthy approach and a precise presentation. How precise do you need to be? A good rule of thumb is to try to get your fly in a dinner-plate-size area around the mouth of a feeding carp. Making consistent casts with that kind of precision takes a lot of practice, but there are a few tricks that will get your fly in the sweet spot with regularity.

Anticipating Carp Movement

Tailing carp move pretty slowly along the bottom in a fairly straight line. They are easy to spot and predict because you can see their tails go up every time they tip their noses down to feed. Cruising carp are a bit more random, but they still follow a pretty straight line as long as nothing spooks them or grabs their attention. Try to anticipate where the fish is going so that you can make a cast and have your fly in place when the fish gets there.

Casting Nymphs and Bottom Streamers beyond the Carp

While a dinner-plate-size target area will provide the best chances of a carp taking your fly, you do not want to drop your fly right on the fish's nose. This is a guaranteed way to spook carp. Instead, cast beyond the fish so that you can retrieve your fly into the carp's path as it approaches your leader. By planning your cast and presentation in this manner, you can pull your fly into the carp's path rather than trying to hit the small target area with a direct shot.

Casting beyond feeding carp and retrieving your fly into the fish's path is a great way to catch carp with nymphs and bottom streamers. This technique allows you to make good presentations to feeding carp without pinpoint casting. It also greatly reduces the chances of spooking the carp when your fly splashes down.

Presenting Swimming Streamers to Carp

Carp do not feed solely on the bottom. They are more than capable of taking baitfish in shallows as well as open water. If you encounter feeding carp that ignore your bottom presentations, they may be eating baitfish.

Present swimming streamers by casting beyond cruising fish and retrieving the streamer into the fish's path. Timing is crucial because you do not want to let the streamer sink to the bottom. Observe the fish, anticipate its direction, cast beyond the fish's path, and retrieve your streamer into the path with short line-strips. Keep a tight line and point your rod tip at the streamer so that you can swim or stop the streamer at will.

Although carp usually stay their course when feeding, they may turn to take a streamer or even briefly chase a streamer before striking it. Tie on a streamer when you encounter carp that are aggressively feeding and putting on a splashy display in the shallows.

It can be hard to get a handle on a big carp, but gloves help. HENRY COWEN

Presenting Dry Flies to Carp

Carp do feed on the surface, though not as often as they do underwater. Carp frequently eat thistle seeds, cottonwood seeds, and mulberries from the surface. Heavy insect hatches or spinner falls will attract carp to the surface as well. Unlike trout, which rise to individual insects, carp will take multiple insects, seeds, or fruit with one rise.

Just like subsurface-feeding carp, surface feeders usually move in a somewhat predictable path. Treat surface-feeding carp with special care because you can spook them with your line, your leader, or the drag on your fly. Try to anticipate the carp's path and put your fly in it. If the carp does not take your fly, wait until the fish has passed before picking up your line so that you do not spook that carp or any others that are feeding nearby.

Strike Indicators

I am a big advocate of strike indicators, both for trout and warmwater gamefish. However, if fly fishing for carp is your game, use strike indicators very sparingly. It is difficult enough to get your fly in front of a feeding carp without spooking the fish. Adding a strike indicator to the equation will increase your troubles exponentially. Fly fishing for carp is almost exclusively sight fishing, so there is really no need for a strike indicator. You are much better off watching your fly, rather than an indicator, for the take. Toss a small indicator in your fly box just in case, but don't plan on using it very often.

HOOKING AND LANDING CARP

Carp can be very subtle when they take a fly. You need to react quickly to certain clues to avoid missed takes. Because you will be sight fishing, it is crucial that you either see your fly or that you know exactly where it is. You can sometimes see the orange flash of a carp taking your fly, but the only sign of a take is just as likely to be the fish tipping its head or raising its tail. Keep your slack line to a minimum so that you can "test" these signals. If you tighten up the line and feel the fish, set the hook immediately with a very solid strip-strike. If you tighten up and the fish is not there, loosen up on the fly line so that the fly can gently settle back to the bottom while the carp is near.

Carp can be very aggressive when taking streamers, and there is little doubt that you will notice this type of strike when it occurs. Watch for the orange flash of the carp's mouth as it attacks your streamer. Keep a tight line so that you can feel the weight of the fish, then strip-strike and hold on.

Carp are tough fish, but should nonetheless be gently released. HENRY COWEN

Hooking carp with a dry fly in still water is fairly straightforward. You are sure to see the carp take your fly on top. When fishing dry flies for carp on rivers and creeks, however, you will have to take slack line into account. Remember, dead-drifting a dry fly requires a controlled amount of slack in the fly line. You will need to pick up the slack before you can set the hook, so keep your rod tip close to the water's surface. Set the hook by raising the rod tip and strip-striking simultaneously to recover the slack line and drive the hook into the carp's mouth.

Running Carp

Have you ever wondered why you need all of that backing on your fly reel? Wonder no more, because you will find out the first time you hook a carp on the fly. Carp are the longest, strongest running freshwater fish that I know of. If you are accustomed to fly fishing for bass or trout, you will be shocked by the tenacity of the common carp.

Carp will usually run as soon as you set the hook. The first run is likely to be long and strong, so let the fish go. Don't tighten your drag to the point that you could break the fish off. Remember, carp are very strong, and you will probably be landing them on the equivalent of 10-pound-test line.

You can start to recover line once the carp has made its initial run. Use your rod to pressure the fish and try to steer it back toward you. If it runs again, you can apply more pressure with your rod and the drag. Rather than try to fight the carp with your rod vertical, try using a low rod angle in the opposite direction that the carp is running. A low, opposite rod angle will tire the fish more quickly. This approach also forces the carp's nose down, often causing the fish to give up faster.

Landing Carp

You can land small carp by simply grabbing them over the back of the "neck" as you would a small northern pike. Big carp can be tough to get a handle on, so use a long-handled net for large fish. If you are going light and hook a large carp without a net, try to beach the fish in very shallow water or on a grassy bank. Be careful that you don't damage the carp's scales if you do this. Carp are pretty robust, but you don't want to hurt them needlessly.

It can be difficult to remove hooks from the thick lips of a carp, so barbless hooks are best. Be sure that you have hemostats or needle-nose pliers handy to help you remove the hook.

Just as striped bass give every freshwater angler a shot at true saltwater gamefish, carp provide the opportunity for saltwater-style sight fishing in nearly any lake, pond, or river across the country. Carp are wholly undeserving of the "trash fish" designation that seems to haunt them. Catching carp on the fly is perhaps the pinnacle of warmwater fly fishing, if catching the most challenging and exciting sport fish on the lightest of tackle is to be the definition of sportfishing. You won't get a reel-screeching run out of every carp that you hook, but those that do run provide the thrill that keeps carp anglers coming back to the flats again and again.

Guide Henry Cowen showing off the fruits of his labor. HENRY COWEN

CARP FLIES

Gold Crazy Charlie

Hook: Mustad 9671 or equivalent wet fly
Thread: Danville's Flymaster 70 Denier
Eyes: Gold bead chain
Body: Krystal Flash
Wing: Brown bucktail

Silver Crazy Charlie

Hook: Mustad 9671 or equivalent wet fly
Thread: Danville's Flymaster 70 Denier
Eyes: Silver bead chain
Body: Krystal Flash
Wing: Gray bucktail

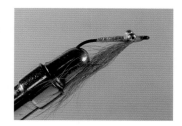

Lead-Eye Crazy Charlie

Hook: Mustad 9671 or equivalent wet fly
Thread: Danville's Flymaster 70 Denier
Eyes: Lead dumbbell
Body: Squirrel dubbing
Flash: Flashabou
Wing: Squirrel tail

Backstabber

Hook: Mustad 9671 or equivalent wet fly
Thread: Danville's Flymaster 70 Denier
Eyes: Bead chain
Body: Dyed squirrel dubbing
Wing: Marabou
Hackle: Dyed hen or webby rooster
hackle

Pheasant Tail Nymph

Hook: Mustad 9671 or equivalent wet fly
Thread: Danville's Flymaster 70 Denier
Tail: Pheasant tail fibers
Rib: Copper wire
Body: Pheasant tail fibers, wrapped forward
Thorax: Peacock herl
Wing case: Pheasant tail fibers

Blue-Winged Olive Parachute

Hook: Mustad 94840 or equivalent dry fly
Thread: Danville's Flymaster 70 Denier
Tail: Stiff hackle fibers
Wing post: Gray turkey flat feather
Hackle: Dun genetic dry-fly hackle
Body: Dry-fly dubbing

CHAPTER 10

Warmwater Fly-Fishing Destinations

If you're like me, you are probably pretty excited to get on the water after learning all about warmwater fly fishing. There is nothing like a good fishing book to get your brain in gear, and I certainly hope it's nice enough right now that you can get out on the water. A big part of warmwater fly fishing is that you can do it almost anywhere. You don't need to drive for hours to get on a good piece of water. Just string up your fly rod and go down to the nearest park, stream, reservoir, or pond.

Of course, there are many prime warmwater fisheries around the country that draw thousands of anglers every year with the promise of fast action and big fish. Just like prime trout waters such as Montana, Colorado, and Michigan, these warmwater hot spots attract both fly and spinning anglers. Unlike some of the more popular trout waters, however, you are not likely to run into elbow-to-elbow angling at any of these prime locations. There are plenty of fish to go around at all of these sensational waters. Now tie up some flies and get out on the water!

LAKE CUMBERLAND

Jamestown, Kentucky

Lake Cumberland and the surrounding area attract over four million visitors every year, but don't let that discourage you if you prefer a little solitude. At 101 miles in length, this is a really big lake. Covering about 63,000 acres, Lake Cumberland has 1,255 miles of wooded shoreline. Just for reference, the entire coast of California, Oregon, and Washington is 1,293 miles long! The lake averages 90 feet in depth, but there are countless bays, cuts, and creek arms to explore with your fly rod.

Lake Cumberland is one of the top reservoirs in the nation for striped bass. There are plenty of guides on the lake who specialize in catching big stripers with gear and bait. If you are going after stripers on Cumberland with a fly rod, be sure to do your homework so that you can identify concentrations of baitfish that are within reach of your fly equipment. You will definitely benefit from a full-sinking fly line because stripers are very likely to be deeper than you will be able to reach with a floating fly line. Flies that imitate alewives and shad will produce stripers on Cumberland.

Though famed for its striper fishing, the real treat for fly anglers on Lake Cumberland are the bass that can be caught along the miles of shoreline. There are miles upon miles of wooded shoreline with rocky bluffs, fallen timber, and submerged points that attract trophy-size largemouth, smallmouth, and spotted bass. This is a deep lake, so you should have a sinking-line outfit in case the fish are deep, but there is a good chance of catching bass with top-water bugs and swimming streamers during the spring, summer, and early fall.

Like many large reservoirs, Lake Cumberland has an excellent coldwater tailwater fishery that features rainbow trout and brown trout. If you get tired of throwing big streamers and bass bugs on the lake, you can always head for the tailwater for a little trout action. You will need to purchase an additional trout license to fish the tailwater, but $10 is a bargain price to get you onto trout water of this quality in the Midwest.

Of course, fly fishing is great, but I know that it is a lot easier to get in a little fishing when you're on vacation rather than trying to squeeze in some vacation on your fishing trip. I'd like to offer up some of my favorite attractions and things to do when you are visiting these warmwater hot spots. Lake Cumberland is only 2½ hours from Louisville and Nashville and about 3 hours from Cincinnati. All three cities offer many attractions that will keep your whole family entertained while you are in the area. Among my favorites are Cincinnati Reds games at Great American Ballpark, the Louisville Slugger Museum and Factory in Louisville, and the Gibson Showcase at Opry Mills in Nashville.

Lake Cumberland is located near Russell Springs, Jamestown, and Monticello in south-central Kentucky. Prime warmwater species include striped bass, largemouth bass, smallmouth bass, spotted bass, and crappie. Prime coldwater species in the tailwater include rainbow trout and brown trout. Fly-fishing guide services are available on the tailwater, but most guides on the main lake specialize in spinning and bait-casting gear. You can rent boats at Lake Cumberland State Dock (888-782-8336, www.statedock.com). An annual nonresident fishing license is $50 or a 7-day license is $30; trout stamps for the tailwater are an additional $10.

DALE HOLLOW LAKE

Celina, Tennessee

Dale Hollow is a short drive from Lake Cumberland, but they are two distinctly different lakes. Dale Hollow features exceptionally clear water and a hard, rocky bottom that make it an incredible habitat for smallmouth bass. In fact, David Hayes's 11-pound, 15-ounce smallmouth that has stood as the all-tackle world record since 1955 came from Dale Hollow. The chance of hooking and landing a world-record bronzeback with fly gear is slim, but that doesn't mean you can't expect some great fly fishing for smallies on Dale Hollow. While deep water commands the attention of spinning-gear anglers, fly anglers should concentrate on shallow structure and cover where flies can be presented more easily.

Focus your fly-fishing efforts on the steep rocky bluffs that surround the lake. There are also many creek arms and shallow bays that offer fly anglers a good shot at bass. Clouser Minnows and baitfish patterns that imitate alewives are a good choice for bass that are feeding in the water column, while Holschlag Hackle Flies, Skittish Crayfish, and Bead-Head Woolly Buggers will pick up bass that are keying on crayfish on the rocky lake bottom.

Dale Hollow also features fine trout fishing in the Obey River below the dam. You can catch browns, rainbows, and even brook trout in this coldwater tailrace.

Dale Hollow is very close to Nashville, so you can definitely slip away for an evening to catch a show at the Ryman or the Grand Ole Opry. Chattanooga, Tennessee, is about 2½ hours away and is the home of the Tennessee River Aquarium. Unlike many public aquariums, the Tennessee River Aquarium has a massive collection of freshwater gamefish like trout, bass, and catfish. I always make a point to stop by when I'm passing through on the way to Florida.

Dale Hollow Lake straddles the Tennessee-Kentucky border near the town of Celina, Tennessee, about 1½ hours from Lake Cumberland. Primary warmwater species include smallmouth bass and largemouth bass. There are also spotted bass and muskellunge in the lake. Rainbow, brown, and brook trout can be caught in the tailwater. Most guides on the lake focus on spinning and bait-casting, but fly-fishing opportunities abound for adventurous anglers with a boat. You can rent boats on Dale Hollow at Sunset Marina & Resort in Byrdstown (800-760-8550, www .sunsetmarina.com) or Star Point Resort (866-782-7768, www.starpoint resort.com). An annual nonresident Tennessee fishing license is $41; 3-day licenses are available for $16.50. You can purchase a 1-day all-species license that includes trout for $16 for fishing the tailwater. Please be aware that Dale Hollow Lake has waters in both Tennessee and Kentucky; while the two states have a reciprocal fishing agreement, you may need licenses for both states to fish some waters.

SUGAR CREEK

Crawfordsville, Indiana

Let's move on to one of my favorites, Sugar Creek in west-central Indiana. I lived in the area for many years and spent many great days on Sugar Creek, where there is a surprisingly good population of large, feisty smallmouth bass. The prime smallmouth areas on Sugar Creek are near Shades and Turkey Run State Parks. The high stone bluffs and picturesque forests of the area are not what most folks think of when they picture Indiana, but you'd be hard-pressed to find a prettier place to catch 20-inch smallies anywhere in the country.

Crayfish patterns rule on Sugar Creek, so be sure to tie up a ton of Holschlag Hackle Flies, Skittish Crayfish, and Bead-Head Woolly Buggers. Concentrate on rocky bluffs, outcroppings, and deep holes for the best smallmouth action. There is a one-fish, 20-inch limit on smallmouth bass on Sugar Creek around the parks, so you can reasonably expect to hook up some hogs. Sugar Creek is a popular canoeing destination, so early mornings, late evenings, and weekdays offer the best fly-fishing opportunities with the least amount of canoe traffic.

Wildcat Creek Outfitters in nearby Zionsville, Indiana, is a top choice for fly-fishing-specific guided trips on Sugar Creek. They offer a complete fly shop, and head guide Scott Gobel will provide you plenty of shots at smallmouth bass on Sugar Creek as well as the nearby White and Tippecanoe Rivers.

You can camp at Shades or Turkey Run State Parks or stay in Crawfordsville. Much of the prime fly-fishing waters on Sugar Creek are within an hour of Indianapolis, so you can even make a day trip from Indy to fish Sugar Creek. Indianapolis is the home of the finest children's museum in the country if you are looking for a place to take the kids. If you are in the area, be sure to check out the Indianapolis Motor Speedway Museum as well. The museum contains the hands-down finest collection of race cars on earth and will delight kids and adults alike.

Sugar Creek is located in west-central Indiana. The river is fishable from the small town of Darlington down to Montezuma. Prime smallmouth areas are in and around Shades and Turkey Run State Parks in Parke and Montgomery Counties. Smallmouth bass are the major warmwater attraction, but panfish also abound and there are some great opportunities to sight-fish for carp. Wildcat Creek Outfitters (317-733-3014, www.wildcatcreekoutfitters.com) offers a full-service fly shop as well as guided trips for smallmouth bass and carp on Sugar Creek. You can rent canoes at Clements Canoes (765-435-2070, www.clementscanoes.com) near Shades State Park. An annual nonresident fishing license is $35; you can also purchase a 7-day license for $20 or a 1-day license for $9.

UPPER MISSISSIPPI RIVER

Minneapolis–Saint Paul, Minnesota

The concrete-lined muddy waters of the Lower Mississippi are a far cry from the prime smallmouth country that defines the upper stretches of

Tim Holschlag of Smallmouth Fly Angler is the king of fly fishing for smallmouth bass, as this Upper Mississippi 21-incher illustrates. TIM HOLSCHLAG

the Mighty Miss as it winds through southwest Minnesota. There is a 12- to 20-inch slot limit with a limit of one bass over 20 inches on the 45 miles of river between Saint Cloud and Dayton. In addition, a statewide no-kill regulation after September 10 of each year ensures that there are plenty of nice bass to go around.

Water conditions on the Mississippi can vary greatly from season to season and even daily on the free-flowing sections of the river. Be prepared for any situation by bringing along plenty of top-water bass bugs, swimming streamers, and bottom streamers in various weights. You should bring a floating fly-line outfit at the minimum and a sinking-line rig if you can.

The Upper Mississippi is big water, but veteran guide and all-around smallmouth guru Tim Holschlag will put you onto fish. Tim is a busy guy, not only guiding but also running Smallmouth Fly Angler in Minneapolis, where he produces instructional videos like *Smallmouth Bass Fishing: Revealed,* writes books and articles, and leads many smallmouth-related schools, seminars, and trips. Tim has also led many great conservation endeavors, with smallmouth bass angling at the forefront of his efforts.

Minneapolis–Saint Paul is a thriving metropolitan area with many attractions. Rock-and-rollers will enjoy the live-music scene in downtown Minneapolis, while the many parks and green spaces around the city provide a more relaxing atmosphere. "The Cities" now have a premiere baseball venue in Target Field, where you can take in a Twins game. If you enjoy scenic drives, check out the view along the Saint Croix waterway from Red Wing to La Crosse, Wisconsin.

In Minnesota, the Mississippi River runs from its midstate headwaters to the Iowa state line. You will want to concentrate on the areas around Minneapolis–Saint Paul and the slot-limit stretch between Saint Cloud and Dayton. Smallmouth bass are the primary warmwater gamefish in this area, but there are ample opportunities to catch largemouth bass, crappies, northern pike, and muskellunge. Contact Tim Holschlag at Smallmouth Fly Angler (612-781-3912, www.smallmouthflyangler.com) for guided trips. An annual nonresident Minnesota fishing license is $45; you can purchase a 1-day license for $12.

HAYWARD LAKE AREA

Hayward, Wisconsin

There is no place on earth that can compete with the angling allure of the "northwoods," and Hayward lies at the heart of it all. This is Musky Country, where you can expect to do battle with the toughest fish that swims in freshwater. The Hayward area is home to dozens of excellent lakes as well as the fabled Flambeau, Chippewa, Namekegon, and Saint Croix Rivers. If nothing else, you'll never run out of places to fish when you are in Hayward.

Muskellunge are the main draw around Hayward, with festivals and tournaments that celebrate the big fish. If predator fishing is not your thing, there is also plenty of great smallmouth bass fishing in the area. Just watch out—you might hook the bronzeback of a lifetime only to land half a fish! Big streamers are the top-producing flies for anglers pursuing muskies and trophy-size northern pike. You can expect good smallmouth action with streamers and top-water bass bugs. Bring your heavy tackle if you are going after muskellunge—you'll need it.

Hayward is the home of muskellunge legend Brad Bohen, and he runs Musky Country Outfitters here. Musky Country Outfitters is the top choice to put you onto big fish. Brad also designs big flies and runs his own brand of fly-tying materials, Primo Tail, from Hayward.

Don't expect big-city excitement when you visit Hayward. This is truly northwoods country, so there is plenty of fishing, camping, canoeing, and hiking to keep the family busy. While you are in the area, be sure to visit the Leinie Lodge in Chippewa Falls, where you can tour the historic Leinenkugel's Brewery year-round and enjoy a cold beer or two.

Hayward is in northwestern Wisconsin, about 2½ hours from Minneapolis–Saint Paul and 4½ hours from Madison. There are multiple lakes and rivers with excellent fly-fishing opportunities in the area. Muskellunge, northern pike, and smallmouth bass are the major warmwater species. Contact Brad Bohen at Musky Country Outfitters (715-558-2937, www.muskycountry outfitters.com) for guided trips. An annual nonresident Wisconsin license is $50; you can purchase a 1-day license for $10 or a 4-day license for $24.

LAKE SIDNEY LANIER

Cumming, Georgia

Lake Lanier is a large reservoir in northeastern Georgia. It is an impoundment of the Chattahoochee and Chestatee Rivers, formed in 1956 by the completion of the Buford Dam. Lake Lanier encompasses about 37,000 surface acres, has 692 miles of shoreline, and a maximum depth of 156 feet. Lanier is one of the best lakes in the country for freshwater striped bass and spotted bass.

When pursuing stripers on big, deep reservoirs like Lanier, locating baitfish and matching them with your flies are the critical points. Clouser Minnows, top-water poppers, and baitfish flies that imitate herring and gizzard shad are excellent choices for Lake Lanier stripers.

Fly-fishing guide and writer Henry Cowen guides for stripers, spotted bass, and carp on Lake Lanier as well as on the Chattahoochee. He has developed many tremendous patterns that match the baitfish on Lanier and consistently hook the biggest stripers. Henry has the equipment and knowledge to put you onto the fish of a lifetime on Lanier.

Henry Cowen is an expert guide, fly tyer, and author who specializes in catching stripers, spotted bass, and carp on Lake Lanier and the Chattahoochee River.

173

Lake Lanier is only about 30 minutes from Atlanta, so there is plenty to do and see while you are visiting. Catch a Braves game at Turner Field or hit one of the many all-you-can-eat catfish houses around town.

Lake Sidney Lanier is northeast of Atlanta, Georgia, near the towns of Cumming and Gainesville. Striped bass are the main attraction, though you will have shots at potential world-record spotted bass on Lanier as well. There is also good crappie fishing and both largemouth and smallmouth bass in Lanier. Contact Henry Cowen (678-513-1934, www.henry cowenflyfishing.com) to book a guided trip for stripers, spotted bass, or carp. An annual nonresident Georgia license is $45.

GRAND TRAVERSE BAY

Traverse City, Michigan

Traverse City marks the invisible boundary that separates plain old Michigan from the mythical "up north." There are plenty of great places to fly fish in the Traverse City area, but a really unique opportunity exists on the rock-strewn flats of Grand Traverse Bay, where you can wade miles of crystal-clear water and sight-cast to carp as they feed in the shallows.

Be sure to pack sunscreen, polarized glasses, and plenty of backing before you venture out onto the flats of Grand Traverse Bay. Crazy Charlies, Backstabbers, and Woolly Buggers are top flies for Traverse Bay carp. There are numerous parks and beaches in the area that allow public access to the water.

In addition to carp, Grand Traverse Bay has a healthy population of smallmouth bass that love to hide on the rocky bottom. Depending on the time of year, you might also have a shot at salmon or steelhead in the bay or on one of the nearby Lake Michigan tributaries. There are numerous opportunities for blue-ribbon trout fishing in the area as well.

Traverse City is a genuine resort town, so there is ample dining and lodging right on the water. There are also many private cabins and

Beautiful scenery, a resort-town atmosphere, and ample fishing opportunities make Traverse City, Michigan, a great place to take the family for fishing and fun.
KYRA PERKINSON

timeshares for rent that can provide you with a quiet section of beach all to yourself. Grand Traverse Bay is over 600 feet deep in places, but there are so many wide, boulder-strewn flats that you could fish for days without setting foot on a boat. When you are in the area, be sure to check out Sleeping Bear Dunes National Lakeshore and take a scenic drive on the Old Mission Peninsula. The many orchards and vineyards in the area are popular as well.

Traverse City is located in northwestern Lower Michigan, about 4 hours from Detroit and 5 hours from Chicago. Carp and smallmouth bass are the primary warmwater game species in Grand Traverse Bay. Rainbow, brown, and brook trout as well as steelhead, chinook, and coho salmon are among the coldwater fish that can be caught in the area. An annual nonresident fishing license is $34 plus a one-time $1 fee for a DNR Sport-card. If you are going to fish for trout or salmon, you will need a trout stamp, which $8. You can also purchase a 1-day all-species license for $7 or a 3-day all-species for $21.

LAKE CASITAS

Ventura, California

Southern California is a pretty amazing place. There are not a lot of places in the USA where you can ski in the mountains in the morning then lounge on the beach in the afternoon. The bass in California are amazing, too. The ideal climate and habitat at Lake Casitas produces very big bass. Consider this: Here in the Midwest a 21-inch bass is a nice fish. The record largemouth bass on Casitas is over 21 *pounds!* If you have ever seen *BASS: The Movie,* you know that they take flies, too.

The best time to catch largemouth on the fly at Casitas is in the spring. Marc Mitrany, the head guide at Ojai Angler Professional Fishing Guide Services, recommends flies that match threadfin shad to catch the biggest Casitas largemouth.

You can camp and launch boats at Casitas, but there is no swimming allowed. While you are in California, be sure to take a day and drive the coast up Route 1. I've been down a lot of roads, and this one is definitely one of my favorites. Death Valley, Joshua Tree, and Channel Islands are very popular national parks in the area. If you are exceptionally brave, you can venture down to Los Angles and Hollywood, but I prefer the desert and mountains myself!

Lake Casitas is located in Southern California near the town of Ventura. It is about 1½ hours from Los Angeles and 6 hours from San Francisco and Las Vegas. Largemouth bass are the primary warmwater quarry, though there are nice panfish and trout in the lake as well. Contact Marc Mitrany at Ojai Angler Professional Fishing Guide Services (800-572-6230, www.ojaiangler.com) to book a trip. You can purchase a 1-day nonresident California fishing license for $14.61 or a 10-day license for $45.93.

ACKNOWLEDGMENTS

It's my name on the cover, but I owe a debt of gratitude to many professional guides, photographers, anglers, and friends for their help with this book. Thanks to Henry Cowen, Steve Walburn, Tim Holschlag, Brad Bohen, Jim Klug, Allen Jones, Rich and Kathy Knight, Chris Leininger, and Chad Raich for all of your help!

TEACH A KID TO FISH!

It doesn't matter whether you use flies, lures, or worms. When you teach a kid to fish, you are setting them on the right path at an early age, providing them with a great hobby that can last a lifetime, and ensuring that future generations will enjoy the same sport that we do. Teach a kid to fish!

RECOMMENDED READING

I love fishing books and have collected a nice library over the years. Many of them are specifically about fly fishing, but you can also learn a lot about catching fish from books that don't even mention flies. Here are some of my favorites that I recommend you check out, too:

Bass Bug Fishing by William G. Tapply (Globe Pequot Press, 1999)
This is an absolutely wonderful book about tying and fishing bass bugs by one of the great fly-fishing writers of our time. There are lots of good information here, but *Bass Bug Fishing* is also a great book to read in the Lazy Boy while you enjoy your favorite beverage!

Carp on the Fly: A Flyfishing Guide by Barry Reynolds, Brad Befus, and John Berryman (Spring Creek Press, 1997)
I don't know if this is the first book solely dedicated to catching carp on the fly, but it is definitely one of the best! It even features a special section written by Dave Whitlock about his favorite carp flies.

The Complete Book of Bass by Dick Sternberg (Cy DeCosse, 1996)
Although it is lean on fly-fishing content, this book is a treasure trove of information about all kinds of bass, from largemouth and smallmouth bass to stripers, spots, and white bass. Like many Dick Sternberg titles, it also features in-depth information about many prominent bass lakes and rivers around the country.

Crappie Wisdom: An In-Fisherman Handbook of Strategies by Al Linder (In-Fisherman, 1994)
I don't make any secret about how much I like crappies, and this is the crappie bible. There is not much mention of fly fishing, but you will learn everything you need to know to catch crappies throughout the year.

Fly Fishing in Salt Water by Lefty Kreh (Nick Lyons Books, 1986)
This saltwater title has a lot to offer for sweetwater anglers. Aside from a lot of great striped bass information, the bonefish section features lessons on stalking bonefish that translate well to the carp flats. Of course, this one also features some great fly-casting advice that will help you out on any water.

Freshwater Gamefish of North America by Dick Sternberg (Cy DeCosse, 1996)
This is the place to go when you need the facts about bass, panfish, pike, muskies, stripers, and more. It covers the biology, habitats, ranges, and food sources for dozens of popular freshwater fish across North America.

How to Catch Pike & Muskie by Dick Sternberg (North American Fishing Club, 2000)
There isn't a whole lot in here about fly fishing, but you can't beat this one for information about the habits and habitats of northern pike and muskellunge.

L.L. Bean Fly Fishing for Bass Handbook by Dave Whitlock (Lyons Press, 2000)
This book is packed with tackle, flies, and techniques that catch largemouth and smallmouth bass. It includes Dave's "Straight Line System," which really helped me fine-tune my warmwater fly fishing. As a bonus, you get to sit back and enjoy dozens of Dave's wonderful fly-fishing illustrations.

L.L. Bean Fly Fishing for Striped Bass Handbook by Brad Burns (Lyons Press, 1998)
Striper guide Henry Cowen once told me that striped bass don't know whether they live in salt water or freshwater; they just know that they need to eat! Although technically about stripers in the salt, this book contains a wealth of knowledge about the gear, flies, and techniques that you need to catch stripers wherever they live.

Smallmouth Bass: An In-Fisherman Handbook of Strategies by Al Linder (In-Fisherman, 1984)

All of the In-Fisherman books are great, but this one contains a wide scope of smallmouth bass information. It is actually a team effort from the likes of Larry Dahlberg, Doug Strange, Ron and Al Linder, Bob Ripley, Dave Csanda, and Dan Sura. The book mainly focuses on spinning gear and bait-casting, but there is an excellent chapter about fly fishing.

Smallmouth Fly Fishing: The Best Techniques, Flies and Destinations by Tim Holschlag (Smallmouth Angler Press, 2005)

This is the bible for smallmouth bass fly anglers! Tim Holschlag is the best smallmouth fly angler that I know, and his book provides a ton of bronzeback-specific information that is sure to get you plenty of smallmouth action.

INDEX

ABOUT THE AUTHOR

Nathan Perkinson grew up in southern Indiana, where he spent his youth catching bass, panfish, and catfish. He earned a bachelor's degree from Franklin College of Indiana in 1997. He received his first fly rod at age sixteen, and by age twenty-four he was tying flies, making leaders, and using fly tackle almost exclusively. Nathan's fly-fishing articles have appeared in *American Angler*, *Fly Tyer,* and *Flyfishing & Tying Journal.* He currently lives in northern Indiana, where he fly fishes for warm-water species as well as trout.